Victorian Convicts

Prisoners being escorted to gaol c.1861. (*Authors' Collections*)

Victorian Convicts

100 Criminal Lives

Helen Johnston, Barry Godfrey,
and David J. Cox

PEN & SWORD
TRUE CRIME

First published in Great Britain in 2016 by
Pen & Sword True Crime
an imprint of
Pen & Sword Books Ltd
47 Church Street
Barnsley
South Yorkshire
S70 2AS

ISBN 978 1 47382 373 0

A CIP catalogue record for this book is available from the
British Library

Typeset in Ehrhardt by
Mac Style Ltd, Bridlington, East Yorkshire
Printed and bound in the UK by CPI Group (UK) Ltd,
Croydon, CRO 4YY

Pen & Sword Books Ltd incorporates the imprints of Pen & Sword
Archaeology, Atlas, Aviation, Battleground, Discovery, Family
History, History, Maritime, Military, Naval, Politics, Railways, Select,
Transport, True Crime, and Fiction, Frontline Books, Leo Cooper,
Praetorian Press, Seaforth Publishing and Wharncliffe.

For a complete list of Pen & Sword titles please contact
PEN & SWORD BOOKS LIMITED
47 Church Street, Barnsley, South Yorkshire, S70 2AS, England
E-mail: enquiries@pen-and-sword.co.uk
Website: www.pen-and-sword.co.uk

Contents

Introduction to the Convict Prison System

T he convict prison system was established in Britain from the 1850s onwards partially in response to the ending of convict transportation to Australia. During the first half of the nineteenth century discontent with the convict system grew in Australia, and colonies there refused to take anymore convicts sent out from Britain. Eventually the British state conceded that a new system would have to be developed and that people sentenced in Britain would be securely held 'at home' until they were released. In all, ninety prisons (for both serious and minor offenders) were built or added to between 1842 and 1877. Joshua Jebb, then Surveyor-General and later Director of Convict Prisons, designed a system of penitentiaries that were administered and managed by the government and which would hold all offenders sentenced to long custodial terms. When transportation was removed as a sentencing option for the courts, it was replaced by 'penal servitude' (Penal Servitude Act 1853). Instead of a set number of years banished to countries overseas, inmates would serve a shorter period of penal servitude inside a convict prison on the British Isles. For example, seven years' transportation was replaced with four to six years' penal servitude. During the early years of the convict prison system approximately 10,000 offenders were sent out to Western Australia at the request of colonists there, but this ended in 1868. From that time on all serious offenders, with the exception of those sentenced to death, served periods of long-term imprisonment in the UK. The sentence of penal servitude lasted for nearly 100 years as part of the criminal justice system and left an enduring image of British imprisonment on the popular consciousness. The 'convict' shackled and at work on the moors, or clothed in the uniform with 'broad arrows' or 'crow's feet' identifying them as government property and impeding their escape, is often the way in which popular culture remembers Victorian imprisonment.

The sentence of penal servitude was made up of three sections: the first was a period of separate confinement, then a period on the Public Works and then, subject to conditions, release on licence. Initially, the minimum sentence of penal servitude was four years: one year in separate confinement and three years on the Public Works. Separate confinement was a regime of isolation during which prisoners were prevented from having contact and communication with other inmates; they were held alone at all times, labouring, sleeping, and eating in their cells. Male prisoners worked at tailoring, weaving, shoe, bag or mat-making, picking oakum (tarred rope used for caulking ships) and female convicts undertook needlework and knitting. Convicts came out of their cells to attend chapel and to go to daily exercise; during such time they would have had silent association with the other prisoners. Millbank and Pentonville prisons in London were both used for the separate confinement of male and female prisoners and after Millbank closed in 1890, Wormwood Scrubs was used instead. The government also rented cells from local prisons, for example, at Wakefield in England and Perth in Scotland, where convicts underwent a period of separate confinement. After completing separate confinement, prisoners moved to the Public Works or convict prisons.

The longest period of the penal servitude sentence was spent on Public Works, and, as the name suggests, prisoners were put to labour here for the benefit of the public. All of the convict prisons were in London and the south of England. Male prisoners on Public Works were held in Brixton, Chatham, Chattenden, Dartmoor, Dover, Lewes, Maidstone, Parkhurst, Portland, and Portsmouth. Female prisoners underwent Public Works at Fulham Refuge and at Woking Prison for most of the nineteenth century; both Parkhurst and Brixton had housed women in the early years of the convict system but both were used only for short periods of time. In the 1890s, Aylesbury Prison started to take female prisoners and during the 1920s and 1930s, female convicts were also sent to Liverpool and young women to borstal training at Aylesbury. Convicts worked at building docks and sea defences, on excavations, in quarries, or they made bricks and cleared moorland. There were other superior jobs such as blacksmith, carpenter or work in the bakery. Those who were unable to undertake such heavy work were put to labour on farms and women were employed in the laundry (most of which was for the whole convict system) as well as in knitting and needlework.

Convicts worked in association i.e. alongside each other at labour, though communication was strictly regulated to what was necessary for work. At night convicts would sleep and eat in separate cells. The internal regime also encompassed what was called the progressive stage and marks system; as the name suggests convicts progressed through stages based on time periods and they earned marks. They were required to meet a certain number of marks each day in order to progress to the next stage. Prisoners worked through stages from probation to third, second, first and then to special stage; promotion was based on their good conduct and industry and in the first stages on time served. Convicts earned between six and eight marks per day based on the degree of effort and at each stage would receive small benefits to alleviate their confinement and this might include being able to write or receive a letter, being permitted a visit from a relative, or an extra period of exercise during the week.

The progressive stage system was a 'carrot and stick' approach; marks were earned in exchange for gained better conditions but it was also underpinned by an extensive system of punishments. Stage marks and remission marks could be lost for breaches of the prison rules and regulations and prisoners could be moved back a stage or two. They might be required to earn more stage marks before progressing or they might lose remission marks which would reduce the number of days early they might be released on licence from their sentence. Prisoners were also punished through dietary punishment such as bread and water for three days, or they might be sent to 'close confinement' (basically solitary confinement) or a refractory cell (punishment cell). Women could also be placed in a very stiff and uncomfortable 'canvas dress', whilst men could be made to wear what was known as a 'parte-coloured' jacket (basically a multi-coloured garment that immediately marked them out as wrongdoers within the prison). Both men and women could also be placed in handcuffs, or in more severe cases, in a straitjacket. For the most serious offences against prison officers, male offenders could be flogged.

The final part of a convict's sentence was usually served on licence, and the next chapter explains exactly what this entailed.

The Convict Licensing System

Background

The licensing system introduced for convicts in 1853 had its origins in the development of the 'ticket-of-leave' system by Sir Philip Gidley King, third Governor of New South Wales (1800-06). This system allowed well-behaved transported convicts to either work for themselves or for a designated employer within a proscribed district of the colony before their sentence expired or they gained a pardon. The system was designed to act as an incentive to encourage good behaviour amongst transportees and many thousands received such tickets.

In 1853, following the introduction of the convict prison system as a result of the 1853 Penal Servitude Act, which replaced sentences of more than seven years' transportation with penal servitude, it was decided to introduce a similar system in Britain. The system, known officially as licensing (but popularly retaining the term 'ticket-of-leave' throughout the nineteenth century) was championed by Lieutenant Colonel Joshua Jebb CB, Surveyor-General of Prisons and later Chairman of the Directors of Convict Prisons. He was of the opinion that such a system would be more regulated and reformatory in nature (by means of convicts actively having to modify and maintain their good behaviour in order to gain a licence) than the previous indiscriminate use of pardons to free prisoners after serving about half of their sentences.

This view was endorsed by Captain Whitty, Governor of Portland Prison, who stated that:

The system of wearing conduct-badges on the dress, by which the monthly progress of each convict towards the attainment of his ticket-of-leave is publicly marked, works very satisfactorily, as is evinced by the anxiety of even the ill-conducted prisoners to regain a lost good-conduct mark and the efforts to keep subsequently clear of the misconduct book.[1]

Some prisons took this system of rewarding good behaviour a step further; Dartmoor Prison introduced an internal 'ticket-of-leave' system, by which different colour uniforms enabled well-behaved convicts to join a special class of prisoner who were either let out of the prison during the day to perform outside work (normally clearing unproductive land in order to bring it into cultivation), or to work inside the prison on easier tasks, e.g. feeding and looking after the farm animals.[2]

Jebb also stated in the *Report* that with regard to the release of convicts on such licences, 'it may be confidently stated that the majority will do well', since the strictly regulated system replaced the 'free and easy, lax and demoralising system which formerly prevailed in the hulks'.[3] He anticipated that, based on the contemporary prison population, the introduction of a licensing system would affect between 1,800 and 2,000 convicts per year. His estimate was broadly correct. Between 8 October 1853 and 27 June 1854 nearly 1,000 men were released on licence.[4] Anticipating criticism or fears that the influx of such a large number of offenders back into the community would adversely affect crime rates, he stated that men serving time on hulks had previously been released about halfway through their sentence – and that this had not caused any great problems with recidivism.[5] Jebb was being somewhat optimistic here; numerous newspaper reports of offences carried out by 'ticket-of-leave men' fuelled public suspicion of the system throughout the 1850s and 1860s.

How did the system work?

In general, well-behaved convicts serving seven years would be released on licence after serving three years of their sentence, those sentenced to ten years being released on licence after serving four years. Jebb explained the preparations for the release of such convicts in considerable detail, but the main points were that:

- Each convict could be credited with a small amount of money on a daily basis, which was to be accrued as a result of his industry and good-behaviour. This would be credited to an account which would be given the convict on the day of his release. Jebb stated that the average amount was between £5 and £6 for the first 800 convicts who had been released on licence.[6] This money was held in a Post Office account at the stated destination of the licence-holder. Half was given to the licence-holder upon demand, but the other half could only be reclaimed upon the licence-holder providing subsequent proof of his continued good behaviour.
- Each man released on licence to be given a suit of clothes and a pair of shoes upon his release, together with a Bible and Prayer Book.
- Each man to be accompanied to the nearest railway station by a prison officer, who then gives the former convict a railway ticket to his stated destination, together with a small amount of money advanced out of their future earnings for necessary expenses.
- The licence and a certificate of good conduct to be given to the licence-holder by the prison officer at the railway station prior to departure.

Considerable endeavours to procure employment for the licence-holder were also made; prior to release the prison chaplain would draft a standard letter to prospective employers about a month prior to the convict's release, enquiring about the possibility of the convict's future employment:

Sir,
The Secretary of State being anxious to ascertain the prospect of employment of convicts who from time to time become eligible for release on licence, and with a view to assist them in entering upon a career of honest industry, has requested me to refer to any one likely to afford information, or to promote these objects. I therefore take the liberty of addressing you in the case of ----------- now a prisoner under sentence of ------------- in --------------- to make inquiry as to his prospects of obtaining employment, or the means of support, if liberated on licence. He is in -------- state of health and his conduct during imprisonment has been ------------------. I enclose a form which should be filled up by any one inclined to find employment for

the man, or to support him, if an invalid. A certificate of such person's respectability, and power to fulfil his promise should be duly signed by a magistrate, or the minister of the parish. Whether the inquiries you may be good enough to make may prove successful, or otherwise, I request the favour of your returning the enclosed paper filled up, addressed to the Chaplain of the prison in which the man referred to is confined. The prisoner states that ----------- of ----------- will give him employment or support him, as the case may be.[7]

Conditions for holding a licence

The licence-holder was free so long as they met certain conditions. They would lose the licence if they committed another offence; they were also expressly forbidden from associating with 'notoriously bad characters', leading 'an idle or dissolute life', or having no visible means of support' (and this applied to those licence-holders who were infirm or elderly – they had to prove that someone was willing to support them financially). Any breach of the above conditions meant that the individual would be taken before a magistrate and subsequently returned to his former place of incarceration in order to serve out the remainder of his sentence.

Between 1864 and 1869 all male convicts on licence also had to report on a weekly basis to a police station in his residential district. Following the passing of the 1869 Habitual Criminals Act, any police constable (with the written permission of his Chief Constable) could take into custody (without the need for a warrant) a holder of a licence who was thought to be earning a living through dishonest means. This was repealed by the 1871 Prevention of Crimes Act as it proved impracticable. This Act also made provision that any licence holder who breached his licence in a minor manner (i.e. a misdemeanour) could be imprisoned for up to three months without his licence being forfeited. Any licence holder was also to report his or her address to the Chief Constable of the district in which they were residing. Any male licence holder also had to report to his district police on a monthly basis (this could be by letter rather than in person at the discretion of the Chief Constable). Licence-holders were also to notify any change of residency to both old and new police forces within 48 hours of their change of address, with a penalty of up to one year's imprisonment for failing so to do.

Female licence-holders (who were first released on a conditional licence to Female Refuges, where they stayed for nine months before being released on a full licence) were meant to report once to the police force in the residential district of their respective Refuge, as well as to the Lady Superintendent of the Refuge. They were then under no further obligation to report, but the Lady Superintendent was encouraged to keep an eye on them post-release from the Refuge.

Problems with the system

However, all of the above was how the system was *supposed* to operate; in practice it was rarely administered as smoothly as the regulations and rules suggested. In 1878, Sir Edmund Henderson, Commissioner of the Metropolitan Police, admitted failure with regard to the requirement of male licence-holders to report monthly. He stated baldly that 'we cannot enforce that proviso of the Act and it has become more or less a dead letter with regard to the men reporting themselves'.[8]

There were other problems concerning the investigations of the police into the lives of licence-holders and their habits; although rule 372 of the Metropolitan Police handbook stated that 'when the divisional police are directed to make enquiries respecting licence-holders or supervisees, the greatest care must be taken not to injure them directly or indirectly either with their employers or landlords', it was clear that this rule was not always followed. A former convict gave evidence to the Gladstone Committee (which was commissioned to look into the workings of the convict prison system in 1894) that police officers rarely took the trouble to hide the fact that the person of whom they were making enquiries was on a 'ticket-of-leave', thereby causing them considerable problems if the landlord or employer had not previously known their convict status.[9]

A record was kept each year of those whose licences were revoked as a result of their continued offending, and the results published in annual *Judicial Statistics*. The number of revoked licences remained low, but the extent to which this was due to licence-holders' good behaviour is debatable;

it is clear that once an offender had left prison, it was relatively easy for them to disappear from official oversight if they so desired, especially if they moved to large conurbations such as London. The introduction of photography in prisons (upon entry and release) obviously made it easier to keep track of former convicts, as did the invention of fingerprints in the early twentieth century, but licence-holders could (and did) disappear from the system. However, the system was generally considered to be successful and continues to this day, albeit it in a modified form.

Use of licence folders for genealogists and historians

The licence folders which were created to contain details of the licensees are an invaluable source of family and social history; almost 50,000 such folders of male and female licence holders are available for inspection at The National Archives (TNA) in Kew. At The National Archives, over 45,000 male licence folders for the years 1853–87 are held under the catalogue reference PCOM 3, whilst over 4,000 female licence folders for the same years (with considerable gaps) are held under catalogue reference PCOM 4. Further details of licences issued (for both males and females) can be found in PCOM 6. Many other criminal records can also be found at The National Archives – it is well worth looking at their website www.nationalarchives. gov.uk for further details.

The National Archives, in partnership with various commercial genealogy websites, plan to make all PCOM 3 and PCOM 4 records (together with many other related documents) available online. At the time of writing, over 4,000 folders of female licence holders dating between 1853 and 1871 have been digitised and are now available on Ancestry.co.uk, whilst over 35,000 folders of male licence holders dating between 1853 and 1887 have also been digitised and are now available on findmypast.co.uk.

A wealth of information can be found within the licence folders. Apart from the date and details of offences for which the individual was sentenced to penal servitude, many personal and family details are shown. These can include:

- Age
- Religion

- Education (i.e. degree of literacy)
- Marital Status
- Number of Children
- Next of Kin (including addresses)
- Height
- Weight
- Medical History (including any illnesses suffered or diagnosed whilst in prison)
- Colour of Eyes and Hair
- Distinguishing marks including tattoos and scars, loss of digits or limbs etc.
- Occupation
- Photographs (from late-1860s onward)

As well as the above information, much more can be gleaned from looking into the folders in greater depth; for example, further addresses of family and friends can be found from the record of correspondence both sent and received by the convict, whilst many of their previous offences are often listed, giving important information as to their location at a given date.

The next 100 biographical sketches of male and female convicts released on licence during the Victorian period will hopefully both give you some idea of just how much information can be gleaned from such records, and also illustrate how the life stories of those unfortunate enough to find themselves incarcerated in Victorian convict prisons can help inform us about wider social, political and economic conditions of the time. Many of the entries describe often desperate depredation; poverty obviously being one of the apparent reasons for their descent into crime. Others show a more sinister or acquisitive side of human nature, whilst a few include certain elements of dark humour.

The convicts' biographies are listed in alphabetical order, and the text boxes at the top right of each entry along with the accompanying image at the top left serve to illustrate a particular aspect of their lives. It should be noted that several of the individuals described below received more than one licence during their offending careers; in such cases only the most recent of their licence numbers is given. Finally, historical research, no matter how thorough, is not an exact science; whilst every effort has been made to ensure the accuracy of the entries, minor errors and omissions are inevitable in such an undertaking. We apologise for any such mistakes that may have been made and hope that they are few and far between.

A Note on the pre-decimal currency system

Throughout this book the pre-decimal system of currency is utilised. Prior to decimalisation in 1971, the British currency system was based on the ancient and complex system known as L.S.D. (derived from the Latin *librae, solidi* and *denarii*), more commonly known as £ (pounds), s. (shillings), and d. (pence). £1 was made up of 240 pennies (because a pound in weight of silver originally made that number of silver pennies), twelve of which made a shilling. The penny itself was subdivided into farthings (four of which made a penny) or halfpennies (two of which made a penny). To further complicate matters, there were also other coins of various denominations including half-crowns (worth 2 shillings and 6 pennies) and florins (worth 2 shillings). A guinea (a solid-gold coin) had its worth officially set at £1 and one shilling (i.e. twenty-one shillings) between 1717 and 1816. Another coin, the solid-gold sovereign, ostensibly worth £1, had been in circulation in the mediaeval period, but was withdrawn between 1604 and 1817.

It is extremely difficult if not ultimately impossible to accurately equate monetary values from historical periods to those of the present-day. This is due to the fluctuating relative costs of, and demand for, basic goods and necessities (for example staple foodstuffs such as bread have become much cheaper, whilst property prices have risen exponentially), but a multiplication of somewhere in the magnitude of between 80 and 100 can generally be made to mid-nineteenth century figures in order to roughly estimate their present-day values.

1. Samuel Ainge (born c.1820, Tewkesbury, Gloucestershire) Licence no. A27313/45465

Edwardian Smethwick.
(*Authors' Collections*)

The rise of a capitalist and monetary society as a result of the Industrial Revolution created the opportunity for new types of offences – what we now call 'whitecollar' crime, defined in 1939 by sociologist Edwin Sutherland as "a crime committed by a person of respectability and high social status in the course of his occupation". Ainge was a respectable pillar of society, who wrote letters to newspapers on social issues of the day, was the secretary of a campaigning organisation and an outwardly successful businessman. However, when his fortunes declined in later life, he was ready to risk everything on an ill-conceived attempt at 'white-collar' fraud.

For the first sixty years of his life, Samuel James Ainge led a largely blameless life. In the 1841 census he is listed as a schoolmaster, living with his wife Frances in Stafford. The couple had married the year before, and for the next thirty years he appears to have prospered. He is listed as a commercial schoolmaster in 1849, but by 1855 he appears in the *Post Office Directory* for Stafford as a member of the gentry. By the late 1860s Samuel had set up as a coal and coke merchant in Smethwick. By 1871 he had moved with his wife to the more salubrious area of Harborne in Birmingham, and he appears to have taken an interest in current social and political developments.

He became a staunch advocate for the repeal of the various Contagious Diseases Acts 1864-9, by which women suspected of having a sexually transmitted disease could be arrested, detained in locked hospitals and then forcibly inspected for signs of venereal disease (VD). The Acts were brought about as a result of concern over increasing levels of VD in members of the armed forces, but were the subject of attack by campaigners for women's rights, libertarians and other socially-concerned groups. Several campaign groups were created in order to achieve a repeal of the Acts, including the Midland Counties' Electoral Union for the Repeal of the Contagious Diseases Acts, of which Samuel Ainge was Secretary. In 1873, he published an anti-Act pamphlet entitled *Christians, Moral Reformers, and Politicians: Wickedness and Vice Ought Not to be Regulated, Fostered, and Made Easy and Healthy by Government.*

In 1876 Samuel is listed as a partner in a steam-pump manufacturing business, J. E. Rogers and Co. of Smethwick. The partnership was wound up by mutual consent and by 1881 Samuel had set up a new engineering business with his nephew which employed fourteen people. He had also become Secretary of the Smethwick and District Building Society. It appears that his business interests began to falter in the early 1880s, and in 1883 he was arrested in Queenstown, Ireland, just as he was boarding a steamship bound for America. He was brought back to West Bromwich Magistrates' Court and charged with embezzlement (initially for the sum of £49 10s, but the reported figure later rose to £2,000 – he admitted to at least £500). He was found guilty and sentenced to five years' penal servitude. Ainge served just over four years of his sentence, being released on licence in May 1887. He returned to the Birmingham area, and in the 1891 census he is recorded as a hardware merchant. He appears to have had a late flourish in 1894, when he applied for patent GB189400017A (with fellow inventor Joseph Leake) for an improved design of adjustable spanner. However, this invention does not appear to have made his fortune, as when he died in Aston, Birmingham in March 1901, his will lists his assets at £70 1s. 3d.

2. Samuel Algar (born 1822, Palgrave, Suffolk) Licence no. 55

Norwich Castle and Prison in c.1845.
(*Charles Knight's* Old England. A Pictorial
Museum, *1845*)

Norwich Castle was originally built by William
the Conqueror, and it became a local gaol
shortly afterwards. From 1207 it maintained
a very long history of keeping inside its walls,
debtors, prisoners awaiting trial (like Samuel
Algar), and prisoners serving short sentences.
Only Chester, Lancaster, Lincoln, Oxford, York,
and Norwich had retained their original medieval
character up to the 1860s, and the required
upgrading of these kinds of penal fortresses
to employ new penal regimes meant that their
days were numbered. A new prison for Norwich
replaced the Castle in the mid-1880s.

Samuel Algar spent most of his adult life in Suffolk. He was 11 when his father died, and he grew up to be an agricultural labourer, living in Thrandeston. He appears to have married by 1847, as his first son, William, was born at Hartismere during the last quarter of that year. His first recorded brush with the law occurred in March 1848, when he was charged with larceny at Ipswich Sessions, but he was found 'not guilty'. Fifteen months later, he was not so lucky, being found guilty of trespassing in pursuit of game (again at Ipswich Sessions). He was sentenced to one month's imprisonment. These two court appearances may not have been the only ones made by Algar before 1850; in a subsequent newspaper report he and his fellow defendant are described as 'known as bad characters'.

On 3 July 1850 he committed his one and only major felony; he was charged with John Quinton with breaking and entering a shop at Diss, Norfolk, and stealing a quantity of meat. The *Norfolk Chronicle* of 6 July stated that 'the robbery took place at midnight and fell little short of burglary'. Algar had been committed to Norwich Castle Gaol on 10 June 1850 and after being found guilty of the above offence at Norwich Sessions, he was sentenced to be transported for a period of seven years.

However, in the event, Algar served all of his sentence within England; he was transferred from Norwich Castle Gaol to Wakefield House of Correction on 21 August 1850 (where his conduct was recorded as 'good', before being sent to Millbank Prison on 7 October 1851). His second son, Henry, was born whilst he was at Wakefield House of Correction. On arrival at Millbank Prison his occupation was listed as that of labourer, and it was also recorded that he could neither read nor write. He spent just over a year in Millbank, before being transferred to Dartmoor Prison on 21 October 1852. On 10 October 1853 he was released on licence, having served only three years and three months of his seven-year sentence.

He returned to the family home in Suffolk at Stuston, being recorded in the 1861 census as a labourer, living with his wife Sarah and their three sons. Family life appears to have played a part in his desisting from serious crime, as apart from one minor infraction in December 1870, when he was found guilty of being drunk and fined five shillings and ten shillings costs; he did not trouble the courts again. However, the fact that he was given a week to find the money to pay the fine suggests that his was a somewhat precarious financial existence. The following year he gave evidence as a witness in a trial involving the larceny of three hens in Stuston.

He and his family all appear again in the 1871 census, with all of his sons following in his footsteps as agricultural labourers. His wife Sarah died in 1885 and by 1891 Samuel was an inmate at Eye Union Workhouse, still listed as an agricultural labourer. He died two years later in the first few months of 1873.

3. Moses Annetts (born 1823, Eldersfield, Worcestershire) Licence no. 1

A Victorian romantic tryst. (*Authors' Collections*)

Before the passing of the Theft Act 1968 blackmail was not a legal term. However, the act of extracting money by threatening to expose guilty secrets (especially concerning unwise or foolhardy dalliances such as that of Mr Hall and Moses Annetts' future wife) was often practised. The etymology of 'blackmail' has no connection with letters or the post; rather it dates back to the mid-sixteenth century, when Scottish farmers paid 'mal' – rent or tribute paid in kind to protect their herds from being rustled by unscrupulous individuals. By 1826 the term 'blackmail' was used to describe any type of gain from extortion.

Moses Annetts was christened on 21 December 1823 at Eldersfield, a small village to the south of the Malvern Hills. He was the son of William and Elizabeth and spent much of the rest of his life within the environs of his birthplace. In the census of 1841 he is listed as a male farm servant at Willington Heath, Ledbury, and makes his first appearance in court records three years later, when he is charged with the theft of a dead hare at nearby Forthampton, Gloucestershire. He was found guilty at Gloucester sessions and sentenced to three weeks' imprisonment. On 18 April 1850 Moses appeared before the magistrates at Upton-on-Severn petty sessions, charged with highway robbery and assault on a fellow resident of Eldersfield, Mr William Hall. Mr Hall was a prominent farmer in the area, and he accused Annetts of jumping out from a hedge in Eldersfield and violently assaulting him, at the same time stealing eighteen pence from his pocket. It was alleged that Annetts grabbed Mr Hall by the leg and pulled him off his horse. Annetts' defence was a somewhat unexpected one; he stated that Mr Hall had been caught in a compromising situation with Annetts' wife, Mary Ann, and that he (Annetts) had been promised £50 by Mr Hall to say nothing further of the matter. Annetts stated that he had not received the full amount from Mr Hall, and a meeting had been arranged to settle the matter. Mr Hall denied this, and was also opposed to the granting of bail to Annetts, stating that he would be in fear of his life as a consequence. Bail was however granted, as Annetts' father was a freeholder and substantial householder.

At his trial Mr Hall stated that Mary Ann Poole had married Moses Annett, but had already given birth to two children, both of whom she said were fathered by Mr Hall. He denied giving her money for maintenance of the children after her marriage, but admitted to so doing before her marriage to Annetts. The defence restated Annetts' claims but the jury found him guilty of a felony after a previous conviction, and he was sentenced to ten years' transportation. He was transferred to Wakefield Prison for eleven months, then sent to the prison hulk *Justitia*. He was released on licence after serving only three years and three months of his ten-year sentence.

Moses remained living at Eldersfield for the rest of his life, and did not commit another serious offence after his release, but he appears to have had difficulty controlling his temper; in 1857 he was charged along with his brother John with assaulting Samuel Bundy at Corse, near Eldersfield. He was discharged with a caution, with his brother being fined £5.

Many years later in 1870 he was once again brought before the courts on a charge of assault – this time on a Charles Vine at Eldersfield. The courts do not appear to have found the charge a serious one, as Moses was found guilty but only sentenced to a fine of five shillings and costs at Upton petty sessions. Moses offended once more in April 1882, when he and his brother were both fined five shillings for being drunk and disorderly. He died at the age of 86 in 1909.

4. Julia Ashton (born 1856, Rochdale) Licence no. A44853/7518

Victorian vagrant (*Henry Mayhew, London Labour and London Poor, vol. III, 1861*)

Vagabonds had been a concern to authority since Elizabethan times. The 1824 Vagrancy Act was brought in to control the perceived threat of dissolute demobilized soldiers roaming the land, begging and sleeping out, following the Napoleonic Wars. Julia was unlucky in that, shortly after she was prosecuted for being an incorrigible rogue (someone who cannot be reformed), the legislation was altered so that only those prosecuted four times for vagrancy could be described as 'incorrigible', and treated accordingly. She would then have escaped the year-long prison sentence. The offence of being an incorrigible rogue was eventually only repealed in 2013.

Julie or Julia McDonough aka Ashton was born in Rochdale in 1861. Her father Domenick worked in a factory and her mother Bridget was a washer-woman. Both were Irish-born. Julia was first convicted in 1878, when she was found guilty of stealing money from a person in Salford. That offence is often associated with prostitution, and it may be that is what the authorities considered her to be, for the following year she was convicted of being an 'incorrigible rogue' (someone the law defined as a persistent low-level offender) and sent to prison for one year. When released she was quickly re-convicted of stealing a purse from another person and given another three months. She was also convicted on at least eleven occasions for drunkenness. These short sentences did not deter her from offending, and she was further convicted of the same offence in Salford Quarter Sessions courts in 1884. This time she was sentenced to five years' penal servitude and three years' police supervision following her release from prison.

After a few months she was transferred from Strangeways to Millbank and she took the opportunity to write a letter to a 'friend' William Ashton, c/o Mrs Greenwood, 'Flower Pot Public House' in Rochdale (who later asked not to be a conduit for correspondence). The letter was never delivered, however, since the authorities suppressed it (kept it on file because the recipient was not of good character). The police report on Ashton said that 'Police stated that Julia had been supporting Ashton from the proceeds of prostitution and robbery and that "he is what is called a common bully" [a pimp]'.

The same year a letter that she wrote to a man called 'McDonnell' was also suppressed: 'Police says he was living in adultery with Julia Ashton prior to her conviction and upon the proceeds of her wretched mode of life, his name is not McDonnell, he does not live at the Flower Pot Inn but with another woman of low character and in my opinion he is not a fit person to have communication with the convict.'

Her attempts to correspond with others were also thwarted. After investigation, the police reported that 'Ann McCormack and Samuel Tweedale are two of the worst characters in the borough of Rochdale.' Letters between the prisoner, McCormack and Tweedale were then suppressed in the future.

In 1887, Julia was first allowed to go to the East End Refuge, and then she gained a full licence in June 1887. There were then no further reports of Julia offending, but whether she had given up a life of crime at the age of 31, or if she just changed her name and gave the authorities (and historians trying to trace her down) the slip, is unknown.

5. **John Baines** (born 1854, Borwick, Lancashire) Licence no. A35749/45239

Pentonville Prison gatehouse (*H. Mayhew and J. Binny,* The Criminal Prisons of London and Scenes of London Life, *1862*)

The 'Star class' category of convicts was introduced after the Kimberley Commission 1878–9. The Commission argued that whilst the convict system was sufficiently deterrent in its effects, it failed to reform, or even resulted in the deterioration of first-time or less hardened offenders, who associated with all classes of convict. Therefore 'star class' would select out first-time offenders and keep them apart from other convicts to ensure they were not 'contaminated' in prison, though in other ways the punishment they received was the same. Penal administrators corresponded with the local police for background history to ensure that those selected did not have any contacts with criminal convictions.

John Baines or John Bell Allen was about 29 years old when Manchester Assizes found him guilty of fraud and forgery and sentenced him to five years' penal servitude. John was found guilty of a range of offences committed in the course of his employment at the Barrow in Furness branch of the Lancaster Banking Company, where he had worked as a bank clerk. Over about four years, he had falsified accounts, forged deeds and credit orders in order to pay people he owed after large losses whilst gambling on the stock and shares markets.

John had begun work at the bank in 1871, he came from a middle-class family, was Roman Catholic and could read and write well. In addition to the criminal charges, John was also declared bankrupt. He pleaded guilty to some of the charges through 'his own better feeling'. The Judge took his good background into account when sentencing him to five years and the fact that this was his first offence but stated that as a bank clerk he had betrayed a position of trust; and thus was not an ordinary offender. He had yielded to 'terrible temptation … perhaps greedy to become rich, and perhaps led on and encouraged by others to believe that by engaging in these reckless and wanton speculations he would achieve speedy wealth' *(Lancaster Gazette, 7 July 1883)*.

It is probably not a surprise to learn that John was a good prisoner and on entering the prison system had been assessed as 'Star Class'. Initially he was sent to Strangeways in Manchester, then after four months to Pentonville; and then on to Wormwood Scrubs where he was put to work as a tailor. John spent about six months under separate confinement at the Scrubs and then in January 1884 he was moved to Chatham Prison where he worked as a labourer.

During his time in the convict system, John maintained contact with his family, with frequent letters and visits. John's father was also declared bankrupt and John appeared in the bankruptcy courts as a witness. The newspaper accounts suggested at the very least John's father had knowledge of his fraudulent activities at the bank.

John was released on licence on 21 March 1887 and he did not breach the conditions of his licence. In 1889, he married and started a family with Elizabeth, but in 1890 he was once again declared bankrupt under the name John Bell Allen. The family lived in London for a number of years before later moving to Lancashire. John did not commit any further crimes but evidence suggests the precarious nature of his finances and business activities.

6. Thomas Batty (born 1821, Manchester) Licence no. 58215/23270

In 1853 Charles Dickens describes a marine stores dealer's premises (belonging to a Mr Krook) in *Bleak House*: 'In one part of the window was a picture of a red paper mill at which a cart was unloading a quantity of sacks of old rags. In another was the inscription BONES BOUGHT. In another, KITCHEN-STUFF BOUGHT. In another, OLD IRON BOUGHT. In another, WASTE-PAPER BOUGHT. In another, LADIES' AND GENTLEMEN'S WARDROBES BOUGHT'.
Such stores also often operated as places where illicitly gained goods were fenced with few questions asked.

Marine Stores dealer (*Authors' Collections*)

Thomas Batty's first recorded occupation is that of chimney sweep at the age of 20. In the same year (1841) he married Bridget Prendergrass in their home-town of Manchester. Six years later he makes his first appearance in the court records, being accused of receiving stolen goods (in the form of an iron grid). He is acquitted, but this was to be the first of many such brushes with the law. In the 1851 census he is listed as a dealer in rags, living in Nelson Street, Manchester, with his wife, two children and a house servant. It would appear that he had already made the decision to change occupations in order to better his quality of life. With the benefit of hindsight this appears to have been a retrograde step, as all of his subsequent offending was linked with his occupation of marine store dealer.

In 1853 he was again brought before the magistrates, charged once more with receiving property knowing it to be stolen. Again he was acquitted, and his prison record states that he lived in Nelson Street with his wife and two children, his father was still alive, but his mother was dead, and that he could not read or write. Some five years later, he makes another appearance at court, this time charged in connection with the stealing of forty foreign cow hides, valued at £50. His co-accused is a hawker (mobile trader) named Paul Heywood. Batty received a three-month sentence for his part in the larceny and was incarcerated in Manchester Prison.

In April 1861, Batty (who by now was listed as a marine store dealer) appeared at Manchester Sessions, charged with receiving a cask of oil, and is given a three-year sentence of penal servitude. He served the majority of his sentence at Dartmoor, before being released on licence six months early. He returned to Manchester but appeared to be unable to resist the opportunity of dealing in stolen goods; he was found guilty in 1865 of receiving a large quantity of stolen clothes valued at £170. Sentenced to seven years' penal servitude at Manchester Assizes, he once again served most of his time at Dartmoor Prison, where he was diagnosed with a double hernia.

He offended quite regularly whilst in Dartmoor (his offending being mainly concerned with the illicit possession of foodstuffs), but was still released on a second licence on 7 March 1871, having served five years and eight months of his sentence. His general health on release was listed as 'continues good, rupture as on reception'.

He returned to his wife and family in Manchester, giving his destination as Naylor Street, and does not appear to have troubled the authorities again, having changed his occupation by 1881 to that of a timber salesman. His wife Bridget died in 1879, and Batty appears to have followed her to the grave in the March quarter of 1886.

7. William Beckwith (born c.1789, Harrogate, Yorkshire) Licence no. 135

Plaque marking site of the original
Leeds Infirmary (*Authors' Collections*)

Until his trial for embezzlement in October 1849 (which indeed was his one and only brush with the law), as *The Times* reported on 29 October 1849, Beckwith's 'character was considered unimpeachable'. The Leeds Infirmary was by then a venerable institution, having been founded in 1771 and is still functioning as a hospital, albeit in a new location and building designed by Sir Gilbert Scott in 1869. Bearing in mind Beckwith's deception, the site of the original building became the headquarters of the Yorkshire Penny Bank in 1894. This bank is now better known as the Yorkshire Bank.

William Beckwith was born in Harrogate c.1789. He married Margaret Morrow at Romaldkirk, North Yorkshire on 6 February 1812 and by 1824 he and his family (by this time they had at least one daughter) had moved to Leeds, where he became a publican. In the summer of that year he made his first appearance in a newspaper, as a victim of an assault. A labourer, Robert Walker, took out an advertisement in the *Leeds Intelligencer* of 12 August 1824, issuing a public apology for his assault on William Beckwith and acknowledging that the publication of this apology satisfied Mr Beckwith; and that no further proceedings in regard to the attack would take place. For the next twenty-five years, William Beckwith lived an apparently blameless life as the publican of the White Hart, Briggate, Leeds. In February 1837 he was appointed Secretary of the Leeds General Infirmary – this was a prestigious appointment and Beckwith ostensibly appeared to have been a success in the post. His wife died in the spring of 1841 and in the census of that year, Beckwith is recorded as living with his mother and his unmarried daughter.

It is not clear whether it was genuine ineptitude at accounting or, as *The Times* of 22 August 1849 suggested, 'some unfortunate speculations in railways' that led to his spectacular downfall from respectability. Whatever the cause, in August 1849 (a particularly bad year for the Leeds Infirmary as a result of yet another cholera epidemic ravaging the city), Beckwith was arrested and taken into custody charged with the embezzlement of over

£1,000 of subscription fees of the Leeds Infirmary over a period of three years. Although Beckwith's barrister attempted to claim that his 'deficiencies did not arise from dishonesty of intention'; rather as a result of careless bookkeeping, the Recorder of Leeds stated that he could not lose sight of the fact that 'it was the very good character which the prisoner had borne that had enabled him to commit this enormous crime' whilst employed in a trusted role on the board of Leeds Infirmary. Suspicion had grown over the large amount of subscriptions entered in arrears by Beckwith, and at a meeting of the weekly board on 17 August 1849 he admitted to the Treasurer that he was 'a defaulter to a large amount'. On 25 October 1849 he was found guilty of embezzlement at Leeds Borough Sessions and sentenced to seven years' transportation. However, transportation was nearing the end of its life as a punishment and Beckwith actually spent all of his sentence in England. He was first sent to Millbank, then transferred to the prison hulk *Defence* on 24 July 1850, where he stayed for almost a year until being sent to Dartmoor Prison on 11 July 1851.

Perhaps unsurprisingly, Beckwith proved something of a model prisoner, with his conduct being described as 'good' in all the prisons, and he was released early on licence on 26 October 1853, having served exactly four years of his seven-year sentence. Rather surprisingly, he appears to have returned to the scene of his downfall – his given destination in his licence folder is 'Leeds' – but it not unreasonable to suppose that his daughter still lived in the area and was prepared to give him a home.

8. Joshua Bentley (born 1864, Stepney, London) Licence no. A27968B/ 45303

Thames lightermen (*Henry Mayhew*, London Labour and London Poor, *vol. III, 1861*)

Joshua Bentley came from a long line of lightermen who operated flat-bottomed barges which carried coal and other goods on the River Thames. The occupation was a skilled and dangerous one; the Thames was one of the busiest waterways in Europe and the lightermen had to be both physically fit enough to row the unpowered barges and mentally skilled enough to deal with unpredictable tides and currents. Joshua's apprenticeship was interrupted by his conviction; this meant that he would have had to return to the trade to finish it in order to become a member of the Worshipful Company of Watermen and Lightermen, the guild that controlled and represented the occupation, founded in 1514.

Joshua Bentley came from a long line of Thames lightermen (workers of flat-bottomed barges) from Wapping; his family had operated lighters for well over 100 years before his birth on 18 August 1864 at St George in the East, Stepney. He was apprenticed at the age of 14 with the Worshipful Company of Watermen and Lightermen, following in his father's footsteps, and was all set to continue the family tradition. In 1882 he married Ann Deery and they produced a child, followed by another the subsequent year.

This may have put a strain on their finances, as on 7 March 1883, Bentley appeared at Southwark Magistrates' Court along with five other men, charged with stealing twelve bales of wool on 30 January 1883 from the lighter *Petrel*, worth around £300. The men were remanded to appear at the Central Criminal Court in May. It was found that the wool had been taken off the *Petrel* (which was set adrift), loaded into a stolen van and taken to Foundry Wharf (where one of the accused was a foreman). It was then forwarded on the same day by means of the Great Northern Railway to Halifax, where it was sold for £200. Bentley appeared with three other defendants (it appears that the others had the charges against them dropped) on 30 April 1883, where the Recorder stated that 'the offence was a very mischievous one. Only last year he was informed that a single firm had lost £11,000 worth of goods in this way'. Bentley does not appear to have been in trouble with the law before, but the seriousness of the offence still ensured that he received a sentence of five years' penal servitude.

As a first offender, Bentley was classified as a 'Star Class' prisoner, and his previous employer wrote an unsolicited letter to the governor of the prison, stating that he was previously a very respectable man and had never been in trouble before. Similarly, a report from Scotland Yard stated that officers had known him for ten years and described him as 'middle-class, sober and industrious', but with 'indifferent friends'. These 'friends' may well have led him from the 'straight and narrow'.

The majority of lightermen would have been known to the police as they were often the individuals who helped the Thames River Police retrieve the bodies of suicide victims who had thrown themselves off one of the bridges across the Thames (the river still sees around fifty suicides every year). Bentley's father died in October 1885, and he successfully applied for a visit from his family later that month. On 23 April 1887 he was released on licence, having served four years of his sentence, and he returned home to 28 Green Bank Wapping.

Nothing more can be found about him in the available records, but internet genealogy pages suggest that he may have drowned in the Thames at some point in 1890.

9. Lucy Bernard (born 1834, Yorkshire) Licence no. 3504

Female prison wing, Brixton (*H. Mayhew and J. Binny,* The Criminal Prisons of London and Scenes of London Life, *1862*)

Brixton Prison became Britain's first female convict prison in 1853. Previously it had been Surrey House of Correction. The Houses of Correction forced those deemed inadequate, debtors, and the workless poor to labour on the treadwheel, the crank, and other devices designed to both punish them for their apparent laziness, and teach them the value of honest toil. The convict prison carried on the philosophy that work ennobled, by employing similar labour schemes for female convicts. Arguably, conditions and levels of social control for women prisoners were more controlled and stultifying than for male prisoners.

Lucy Bernard of Staniforth Street, Park, was charged with stealing a black cloth coat '… she was stated to be a known thief, and her bad character had driven from her a very respectable husband … committed for trial'. She must have married young, as she was only 21 when she received three months for that offence in 1855. She got another six months for stealing boots in 1856, and twelve months for stealing brushes the following year. Given her rate of offending, it was not surprising that she was sentenced to her first penal servitude (three years) in 1859, aged 25.

She served her time in Brixton Prison before being released on licence in 1861. Lucy was not out of prison for long before re-offending. The theft of an umbrella in May 1862 was reported in a Sheffield newspaper: 'ONE OF THE INCURABLES … A young woman, named Lucy Bernard, described on the police books as having no home, was charged with a felony … she was seen to take an umbrella from the shop door. The prisoner, who was rather neatly dressed, said she did not remember taking it. She had no home to go to, her husband was living with another woman.'

In 1865, after being released from her three-year sentence of penal servitude, she received seven years more for the theft of an overcoat in Sheffield.

Lucy had a turbulent time in prison, being disciplined for theft, inattention to her work, talking when told not to, and general disobedience. Nevertheless, she was licensed for early release in February 1870. She may then have obtained a job in domestic service in London, and she may well have kept out of trouble for the next thirteen years. Lucy did, however, find herself back in court in 1883. She was gaoled for nine months for stealing a coat in Sheffield; gaoled again in 1884 for twelve months for stealing boots, and another six months in 1885 for theft of a shawl.

The newspaper report gives a clue why Lucy started to steal clothes again after thirteen years of honesty. She was described as a widow, homeless, and in need of charity. She then served a number of years in prison for various thefts of trousers, coats, boots, and a fur-lined shawl, until she died aged 59 in Sheffield. The gap in Lucy's offending career can only be guessed at.

No-one named Lucy Bernard appears in the criminal records for that period, but she may have assumed an alias that the authorities never discovered. However, it seems reasonable that, after an early and prolonged interaction with the criminal justice system partly due to her relationship breaking down (and possibly becoming homeless), she found stability in domestic service, until she lost that job and again found herself unemployed and homeless. The prison then provided a home for her once again.

10. Thomas Bill (born 1799, Ledbury, Herefordshire) Licence no. 268/24/22762

Burglary was a capital offence in the eighteenth century, and nighttime burglary was considered one of the most feared crimes aside from murder. In the nineteenth century, transportation or long terms of penal servitude awaited convicted burglars. Charles Dickens characterized burglars as vicious and violent men (Bill Sikes in *Oliver Twist*, and Magwitch in *Great Expectations*). Later depictions (by journalist Henry Mayhew in the 1860s, for example) portrayed burglars as specialist career criminals who trained hard and carried professional tools of their trade with them. Thomas Bill is however probably more typical of the average burglar.

A burglary gone wrong in Charles Dickens's *Oliver Twist* (*Public Domain*)

Being declared bankrupt in 1827, and spending some time as a debtor in the Kings Bench Prison did not deter Thomas from marrying Elizabeth Archer in Worcester the following year. Children followed quickly and frequently: Thomas Henry was born in 1829, William Robert (1830), John Campbell (1832), Ann (1834), Emily (1837), Charlotte Jane (1838, died 1840), and lastly, Mary was born in 1842. Working as a currier (a leather worker), Thomas traded in the local area (Worcester was a centre of the glovemaking industry), suing his supplier in 1844 for not paying the £28 he was owed. The 1840s were turbulent economic times, and the loss of such a substantial sum may have caused severe problems for Thomas' business. His troubles increased when his wife died in Upton-on-Severn in 1845.

Personal and financial difficulties may then have pushed Bill into a bout of serious offending. In 1847 he was fortunately (for he later confessed to this crime whilst in prison) found not guilty of the burglary of an attorney's residence in Pershore, near Worcester. The jury at Worcester Assizes heard that there had been a long feud between Thomas and the attorney who had provided services for the Bill family in the past (and who had also been sued by Thomas) but there was not enough evidence to convict.

The following year Thomas took a gun from a surgeon's house, and was convicted of burglary at Worcester Assizes; and sentenced to ten years' transportation. He started his sentence at Millbank, before being transferred to the prison hulk *Stirling Castle* moored at Portsmouth. After two years he was then moved to Dartmoor Prison in 1851, and was released on licence in 1854.

He was then back in court in October 1855 for stealing cattle, and sentenced to seven years' transportation at Hereford County Sessions. Again he avoided being sent to Australia, and he served most of his time in Dartmoor, and he was discharged from there on the expiration of his sentence in 1862.

Thomas was quickly re-convicted, again for burglary, and sentenced to ten years' penal servitude at Hereford Assizes in March 1863. This time he did not complete the full term of his sentence, and he was released on conditional licence with seventeen months of his sentence unexpired. Within six months he was re-convicted yet again, for 'larceny after a previous conviction'; and this time he was sentenced to two years' custody and seven years' police supervision, at Hereford County Sessions in January 1871. He never completed this sentence because he died that autumn in prison, aged 72.

11. **Emily Bishop** (born unknown date, Geneva or London) Licence number unknown

Tothill Fields prisoners' clothes room
(*H. Mayhew and J. Binny*, The Criminal Prisons of London and Scenes of London Life, *1862*)

Emily Bishop and her sister Louisa appear to have carried on their life of crime for many years, operating as they did under a number of aliases. However, in 1880 they were recognised by a sharpeyed prison wardress at Tothill Fields, who had served as Recognising Officer at the prison for over 30 years, and who was able to identify the two sisters as old offenders who had previously served time at Tothill Fields Prison in 1858 and 1859 under different names. Identification of prisoners became much easier with the introduction of photographs; the Lady Superintendent of Millbank Prison later pointed out in a letter that "I imagine that there must be portraits of these women on their release from penal servitude".

It is highly unlikely that any of the 'facts' given by either Emily Bishop or her sister Louisa (see next entry) to the prison authorities were true – both women appear to have been consummate liars – they appeared in various courts under a number of aliases and constructed an elaborate false 'back-story' of their lives. They claimed at one time or another to be the respectable offspring of a failed merchant, connected to aristocracy, to be born in Switzerland, and to be genteel ladies operating a drawing academy for children.

Emily and Louisa first appear in the criminal records on 3 January 1854, charged at Brighton sessions with stealing a watch and numerous other items from a shopkeeper. Emily received four months, whilst Louisa was acquitted. They were reported as appearing in 'exceedingly neat attire' and gave the impression of a pair of respectable middle-class ladies, whereas they were in fact extremely gifted and scheming confidence tricksters and thieves.

Their *modus operandi* was a simple one; they would visit a shop or a middle-class apartment, usually dressed in very respectable mourning clothes and one of the sisters would feign illness or a mild indisposition. Whilst the other sister was being shown around the shop or apartment by the unsuspecting victim, the 'indisposed' sister would pocket whatever she could find with regard to portable goods. They would then proceed to pawn their illicitly gained goods. On one occasion, they were found with over 100 pawn tickets in their possession, and on another, Louisa had to be forcibly restrained from eating an incriminating solicitor's letter.

They appear to have carried on their criminal activities undetected for another four years until 1858, when they were both found guilty of felony at Middlesex Sessions and sentenced to twelve-months' imprisonment, which they served in Westminster Prison (formerly Tothill Fields House of Correction). In October 1859 they were once again found guilty of similar offences under assumed names and sentenced to three years' penal servitude, being discharged from Brixton Prison in April 1862. There is then a long gap until their next recorded court appearance in June 1880 at Middlesex Sessions. They were both sentenced to five years' penal servitude and three years' police supervision. After being released on licence in November 1882, Emily reunited with her sister and they both reappeared in court in March 1883, once again charged with similar offences. They both received eight years' penal servitude and five years' police supervision, and were sent to different prisons. Louisa served her sentence at Millbank, Emily at Woking, with Louisa being released on a third licence in 1886.

Emily continued offending under a variety of aliases, being sentenced to eighteen months' imprisonment in Wormwood Scrubs for larceny in October 1894.

12. **Louisa Bishop** (born c.1831, Geneva or London) Licence no. A7912B/7513

Victorian prison matron (H. Mayhew and J. Binny, *The Criminal Prisons of London and Scenes of London Life*, 1862)

The origins of the prison medical service lay in the 1774 Health of Prisoners Act which appointed surgeons to assist the sanitation of prisons and look after sick prisoners. In the nineteenth century Medical Officers were of variable quality. Despite being charged with the care of all sick convicts, they paid attention most to those that contracted infectious diseases, illness that prevented prisoners carrying out their prison work, and malingerers. Because they frequently disputed the severity of prisoners' illnesses, and because anyone found to be a malingerer was severely punished, asking for help from the Medical Officer could be a risky process.

There was some dispute as to whether the person convicted under the name Kate Nash on 20 October 1859 at Middlesex Sessions for stealing a cup and saucer, a reticule and other articles was the same woman convicted the previous year as Louisa Bishop. The matter was resolved by the recognising officer at Westminster Prison, a man who had been in the prison service for thirty-four years, who confirmed that they were indeed the same woman. The prison record that was created when she started her three-year sentence actually recorded her under her real name of Louisa Bishop. She served her time and was released on licence from Brixton Prison to Montague Square, London.

Although her records stated she was a Londoner, the 1861 census stated she was born in Geneva, and that she had formerly been an art teacher. Possibly the addition of a Swiss nationality gave her a credibility with potential employers, for she seems to have had a settled period in her life, with no re-offending until 1880. Then she was given five years' penal servitude for stealing silk worth approximately £80.

Not for the first time, in 1882 she reported that her phthisis (tuberculosis of the lungs, causing atrophy and general weakness in the patient) was debilitating. The prison Medical Officer agreed that she was weak, but he was hopeful that her health would continue to improve. Louisa herself was unconvinced, and petitioned the Secretary of State, praying for nine months' remission for herself and her sister Emily on account of their ailing health. The Medical Officer was consulted, and confirmed that she was suffering from phthisis): 'I find from the infirmary record that she has spent a considerable part of her sentence in the infirmary and she is thin and very weak, I am not able to say that further imprisonment would shorten her life.' Whether his medical opinion was valued or not, Louisa was released on conditional licence with nearly three years of her sentence unexpired. However, less than a year after her release she was re-convicted for larceny in a dwelling house and received eight years' penal servitude and five years' police supervision.

Whilst on this sentence, in 1885, she was punished for making a great noise outside the infirmary, declaring that this was the fifth doctor who had been told lies about her by the prison officers, and that the wardens were a bad, deceitful lot. She further alleged that the Matron had been laughing at her saying that 'she should be found dead in her cell like those two women who died from want of nourishment'. She went on to complain that she had been dangerously ill the previous night but had not been visited by the Medical Officer. Indeed, Louisa and various medical officers regularly disputed the extent of her illness until she was released on licence in 1886 and was reunited with her beloved sister Emily.

13. Mary Brannan (born 1843, Dublin) Licence no. 44027/7486

Sheffield Workhouse Token 1815
(*Authors' Collections*)

Sheffield Workhouse came to national attention after a scandal in 1882. John Wood, a 36-year-old draper was seriously ill with consumption and was moved from a lodging house to the workhouse as death was imminent. A few days after his passing, his wife came to view the body but found his coffin screwed down. After insisting the coffin be opened they found the body of an old man named Ellis. Wood's body had been taken to the School of Medicine and was found in the dissecting room. The body was returned promptly but Mrs Wood did claim that his head and face had been shaven and there were marks on the neck. The governor claimed a dismissed employee had switched the labels on the bodies in the dead-house.

Mary Brannan was in her mid- to late-twenties in May 1871 when she received a seven-year sentence of penal servitude and police supervision from Sheffield Sessions for stealing a counterpane. Mary had a couple of previous convictions for stealing boots. Born in Ireland, she moved to Sheffield and worked as a silver buffer.

After her arrest, Mary had been committed to Wakefield Prison to await trial, she was in the early stages of pregnancy and so after the trial she remained at Wakefield until the birth of her child on 15 November 1871. Sadly, the child died a few hours after the birth. In February, Mary was sent down to Millbank, she wrote to her husband James and to her mother but did not received any replies. In October 1872 she was moved to Woking Prison where she worked as a laundress and knitting and needlework. She also wrote to Father Nugent at the St Ann's School in Liverpool. The penal record states she had two children; it is possible that her children may have been at the school.

Mary was a fairly good prisoner, she was admonished a couple of times for quarrelling and knitting stockings for her own use. She also lost three lots of remission marks for shouting and insolence, quarrelling whilst in the infirmary and for working carelessly and being impertinent when checked. She wrote again to her husband and to her mother and this time she did receive replies. She was released on licence to the East End Refuge in May 1875, three years of her sentence remaining and from the refuge in February 1876. However, by the summer, Mary was back in prison, her licence revoked for larceny and being a reputed thief. Initially she was sent to Millbank again, but when it was found she was pregnant, she was moved back to Wakefield Prison, she was released on second licence in November due to her pregnancy.

Two weeks later, in December 1876 Mary was committed again to Wakefield Prison, charged with stealing a pair of boots and due to her previous convictions, she was sentenced to ten years' penal servitude. Mary had spent some time with her baby at Wakefield and then in January of 1878, she was sent again to Millbank; and the baby placed in the workhouse. The medical report from Wakefield reported that Mary had threatened to commit suicide and due to this she was placed in association at Millbank. She was moved on to Woking Prison in March where she worked as a cleaner. She wrote to the Governor of the Sheffield Workhouse about her child and received replies from him. She spent periods in the infirmary due to chest bronchitis and committed a couple more prison offences. In February 1886, she was received at Fulham Prison and then in August was released on licence to be at large, eighteen months of her sentence not served.

14. George Brasher (born 1830, Wilton, Wiltshire) Licence no. unknown

Port Arthur Convict Settlement (*Authors' Collections*)

Van Diemen's Land operated as a penal colony between 1803 and 1853, receiving convicts sentenced in the courts in Britain and Ireland. The island, south of Australia, was established in its own right in 1825, though had been inhabited by Aborigines for thousands of years before. Larger numbers of convicts were sent there from 1840 after New South Wales refused any more criminals. This continued until the last convict ship arrived in 1853. Across this period around 75,000 convicts were transported to the island, the majority of whom were male offenders. They were held at various penal stations, notably Port Arthur, infamous for its chain-gang labour. In 1856 it became known as Tasmania.

George Brasher was born in Wilton near Salisbury in 1830. When George was 10 years old his father, James Brasher was sentenced to seven years' transportation after being convicted of stealing corn. His mother had also been accused but was acquitted of the charges. James was held on the York hulk, he was 39 years old, a labourer and had been convicted several times before for misdemeanours. James was sent to Van Diemen's Land (Tasmania) on the convict ship, *Tortoise* and landed on 19 February 1842. Like many transported convicts, James never returned home; he left his wife, Ann and his three sons in England and set up a new life in Tasmania. James later married again and had ten children in Australia.

In England, George first appeared in court charged with larceny in 1842, but no bill was found (meaning that there was thought to be little chance of conviction should the case be heard). Four years later he was sentenced to one month in prison and was whipped for larceny. In 1848, George was convicted again of larceny. His accomplice, Edward Holloway, received one month in prison but George was sentenced to six months by Southampton Sessions.

In Salisbury, his mother, Ann had been finding life difficult, she had been hawking goods around the town and in September suddenly collapsed and died. The *Hampshire Advertiser* reported that she 'had been living in the lowest state of poverty, and was known as the mother of a wretched family of children, each of whom had been convicted as felons, and also as the wife of a transported convict' (16 September 1848). Ann had been trying to sell laces and stockings in the Elephant and Castle public house and after an altercation over price with a customer, she left the pub slamming the door; she was found to be sober. A short time later, William Rose saw Ann collapse face first in the street, he went to her assistance but she was dead. She had previously had treatment in the Infirmary for heart disease and this was the likely cause of death.

Whilst George was in prison, his brothers, Thomas and Henry, were 'running about town, continuing in practices of thieving and blackguardism, and only waiting for the eye of detection to be cast into prison' (ibid.). A year after George's release from prison he was once again in court. Another larceny charge, stealing linen from a dwelling house, resulted in a heavier sentence; he was sentenced to seven years transportation. George spent three months in separate confinement in Salisbury Gaol and a further ten months' separation at Millbank before being moved to the hulk *Warrior* in March 1851. George was never sent out to Australia and after serving just over half of his sentence on the hulk he was released on licence. In the early 1860s, he was working as a blacksmith and lodging in Fovant, Wiltshire. He died in 1883.

15. Emily Brennan (born c.1843, Whitechapel). Licence no. 97839/ 7619

East End House in Finchley, North London was bought by the Sisters of the Good Shepherd in 1864 and operated until 1948 as a refuge to support distressed Roman Catholic women. It was also known as the Refuge of the Good Shepherd. The refuge was used extensively by the female convict system in the 1870s and 1880s. The 1881 census shows that there were 31 nuns, one lady-boarder, one male gardener, 81 female prisoners and 135 females of the penitentiary (convicts) were living there. By the end of the century, the home no longer received female convicts on conditional licence but instead supported 'poor penitents' and younger girls. The Sisters still live in the original building.

Emily Brennan aged c.38
(*The National Archives*)

Emily Brennan was from Whitechapel, London; she married Thomas in the 1870s but her criminal career had already started. She had had one child previously, Mary Brusher, who was born in the East Indies in the late 1860s. Emily committed a number of offences in her late twenties and early thirties; and received prison sentences varying from three months to eighteen months for the felonies. In 1875 she gave birth to a son, Thomas whilst in prison. In November 1876 she was sentenced to seven years' penal servitude for attempted shoplifting. Emily was in Westminster Prison until transfer to Millbank in June 1878. She regularly wrote and received letters from her husband and was anxious to find out about her baby. She also received visits from a female friend and a little boy who may have been another of her children (her penal record states three children in total). She was transferred to Fulham Refuge in August 1879 and in October 1880 released on conditional licence to Russell House Refuge where she stayed until July 1881.

The census in 1881 shows that her son Thomas, aged 5, was living with her husband in a lodging house in Whitechapel and her elder daughter Mary was living at a Soldiers' Daughters' Home in Hampstead (founded to relieve families of soldiers of the Crimea War).

Only three weeks after her release from the refuge Emily was back in court, charged along with Annie Cohen of stealing £15 and 5 shillings worth of satin, she was again sentenced to seven years' penal servitude. She spent about a month at Westminster and was then sent to Millbank. Again she wrote and received letters from her husband and was visited by a friend and her son. Emily was transferred to Fulham in April 1887. In the intervening years her daughter Mary was staying at Princess Mary's Village Home and she wrote and received a visit from her. She also tried to get her youngest son into the Dr Barnardo's Home. Evidence shows that he had for at least some time been in the care of a family called Walters who adopted him as their own and this had avoided the need for him to be sent to the workhouse. Correspondence suggests that the Walters refused to give up the child, though in 1886 he was admitted to Barnardo's. Now in her mid-40s, Emily suffered from debility and was placed in the infirmary and given a diet of fish or chops, eggs, butter, potatoes, milk and coffee.

She was released again on licence in April 1887 and went to the DPAS (Discharged Prisoners' Aid Society) for support before going to a friend on Brick Lane. A letter from Barnardo's in her file stated that Thomas had been found a good home in the country and was doing well. We lose trace of Emily after she was released, though she does not appear to have committed any further crimes.

16. Lucy Brent (born c.1849, Lincolnshire) Licence no. A35227/7528

The inmates of this house are women who have undergone penal servitude, and on discharge from convict prisons are received here to earn a character. Inmates must do all the work required of them in order to earn their food. No intoxicating drink allowed.

Inmates can have no money in their possession.

Purchases can be made to the extent of each woman's allowance, at the discretion of the Superintendent.

Inmates are only to go out and come in by leave of the Superintendent.

Any woman coming in intoxicated, or refusing to obey the rules, will be summarily dismissed.

(*Rules of Nine Elms Laundry c. 1870*)

Lucy Brent is listed in the 1871 census as a single dressmaker, living in a lodging house in Shoreditch, London. Two years later, on 7 April 1873, she made the first of many appearances in court, being charged at Thames Police Court with assaulting a police constable. She was sentenced to six months' imprisonment.

This doesn't appear to have mended her ways, as within a fortnight of her release she was once more before the magistrates at Thames Police Court charged with the same offence (it is not recorded if the same police constable was the victim). Again she received a sentence of six months' imprisonment. On 24 July 1879 she was back before magistrates, this time charged with wilful damage to a plate glass window valued at £20. She was sentenced once again to six months' imprisonment. Lucy appears to have stayed out of trouble for a short while, but on 26 March

Lucy Brent was brought up as a Roman Catholic but when asked her religion upon reception into prison, stated that she was a Protestant. She subsequently petitioned to have her recorded religion changed back, saying that "she entered prison as a Protestant from a mistaken idea as to prison treatment [...] I am really a Roman Catholic. I am very unhappy having denied my religion and I was given to understand the Catholics was [sic] badly treated, another reason was I wished to go to Nine Elms Laundry at the expiration of my sentence." The Nine Elms Laundry was founded in the 1860s by the Discharged Female Prisoners' Aid Society, a largely Protestant organisation, in order to provide a home and paid work for them upon release from convict prison.

1883 she appeared at Worship Street Police Court, charged with maliciously wounding a fellow lodger, Mary Ann McCarthy, with a knife.

Newspaper reports remarked that her 'appearances during the last sixteen years at this court have been frequently recorded', and that 'something like fifty previous convictions were proved against her', suggesting that she may have committed many more otherwise unrecorded offences (possibly under an alias). Lucy apparently lodged with the victim in a common lodging house in Spitalfields and during an argument, picked up a knife from the mantelpiece and struck her in the arm with it. Due to both the serious nature of the attack and her poor previous record, the Assistant Judge at Middlesex Sessions sentenced her to five years' penal servitude.

Lucy's temper does not appear to have been improved by her involuntary confinement; she threatened to kill the Matron of the infirmary, and also frequently attacked and quarrelled with other prisoners; and was briefly detained in a straitjacket. A letter from the Medical Officer dated 9 April 1885 stated that 'I would like her to remain in the jacket – special instructions will be given to Miss Loader (a nurse) as to its continuance or its removal – I will further report to you when she has been a few days under observation'. The same Medical Officer also stated later that 'I find no traces of insanity proper in her case, but she has a very violent and almost uncontrollable temper'. Despite her outbursts, Lucy was still released early on licence on 16 October 1866 and achieved her wish of being sent to the Nine Elms Laundry in Wandsworth. She subsequently disappears from record.

17. **Lovick Ansted Brown** (born 1830, Taverham, Norfolk) Licence no. 87603/22516

Lovick was clearly a chancer, always looking for a way to make a quick profit. He befriended (presumably with an eye to the main chance) the eccentric William Frederick Windham (left), who owned Felbrigg Hall in Norfolk, and who had been the subject of a scandalous insanity trial in 1861. Windham had married a notorious courtesan, Agnes Willoughby, and bestowed an annuity of £1,500 on her. His family was horrified by the match, and his uncle managed to get a Commission in Lunacy to investigate the sanity or otherwise of his nephew, who unkindly became known as 'Mad Windham'. Whilst he was undoubtedly eccentric (one of his favourite pursuits was dressing as a Metropolitan Police officer and patrolling the beat in Haymarket), the court found him sane. The marriage did not last however, and 'Mad Windham' died in 1866.

'Mad' Windham
(*Authors' Collections*)

Lovick Ansted Brown was the son of publicans who kept the Papermakers' Arms in Taverham, Norfolk. By the age of 24, Lovick had followed in the family footsteps, being recorded as the landlord of the St George's Tavern in Great Yarmouth. In the same year (1854) he married Susanna Groom. He first appears in court records as the victim of a theft from the bar of his new public house; on 7 May 1856 a William Watcham stole six shillings and two pence from the till of the Victoria Gardens public house, and was gaoled for two months.

Lovick appears to have been a happily married man, having two children, Lucretia and Mentor (named after Lovick's father), but in 1862 his wife died unexpectedly at the age of 38. Whether or not this event played a part in his subsequent decline from middle-class respectability is unknown, but in August 1866 Lovick was accused of being an undisclosed bankrupt, owing a creditor over £60. He had certainly become something of a local celebrity, earning the nickname 'Count Brown' as a result of his 'fancy' way of life and his friendship with the eccentric owner of nearby Felbrigg Hall, 'Mad Windham' – he was described as being 'on rather intimate terms with the late Mr William Frederick Windham towards the close of the life of that unfortunate young man'.

His creditor was however forced to hold off bankruptcy proceedings, as at the time Lovick had being held in Norwich gaol since 31 March 1866, charged with receiving stolen goods (five pairs of boots and 62lbs of tobacco belonging to the Great Eastern Railway company). Lovick was found guilty of the crime, along with three employees of the railway company, and sentenced to five years' penal servitude at Norwich Sessions on 6 August 1866.

Lovick committed a number of minor offences, before being released on licence, with one year's sentence not served, on 30 August 1870. He returned to Norwich, and in the 1871 census is listed as a widowed barman. Three years later he remarried and moved to London, being listed as a 'contractor' living in Camberwell. In the 1881 census Lovick is listed as a 'tramway contractor'.

He appears to have rekindled his interest in speculative business concerns, being listed in 1895 as a director of an ill-fated company created to refurbish the failing Metropole Hotel in Scarborough. On 20 July 1897 a Law Notice appeared in the *Standard*, stating that the company had been wound-up. Lovick died in early 1900 at Stoneham in Hampshire, but is buried alongside his first wife, Susanna, in Norfolk.

18. Maria Cain (born c.1841, Galway) Licence no. 52976

H.M. Coroner's coat of arms
(*Authors' Collections*)

The office of Coroner was established in 1194 and the role of a coroner evolved from a financial guardian of the Crown to judicially investigate sudden, unexplained, or unnatural deaths. Coroners remained officers of the Crown until 1888 when the position was appointed by the County Council. The coroner had the power to assemble a jury (until 1926 usually consisting of between 12 and 24 men). This jury was used to determine the cause of death, rather than the guilt or otherwise of a particular suspect of suspects, but they could commit a person to stand trial on suspicion of causing the death. Perjury before a coroner's court was considered to be as serious as before a judge.

Maria Cain (maiden name unknown) was born in Galway, but by 1866 was living in Liverpool with her husband James (aka Patrick). In October 1866 she was found guilty of malicious wounding at Liverpool. She and her husband, together with another married couple, violently attacked plasterers Patrick Coffee and Thomas Maloney in Rose Place, Liverpool. The two victims had been drinking with a blind man named Burns, who lived opposite the Cains and who had previously accused the Cains of robbing him. They accompanied Burns back to his house and Maria saw them, shouting 'Here's one of them in his shirt sleeves, that he has brought to beat us all!', thinking that this was a planned revenge attack on behalf of Burns. Maria and her accomplices violently attacked Coffee and Maloney with pokers, causing them serious injury. All were sentenced to twelve months' imprisonment.

Maria stayed out of trouble for another nine years, but on 4 December 1875 she appeared at Liverpool Assizes charged with two counts of perjury. On 21 May 1875 Maria had given evidence against her neighbour, Jeremiah Cash, stating that he had attacked Winifred McCabe (another neighbour) on 25 April 1875 with a cleaver, causing her subsequent death on 20 May 1875. She stated that Cash had been involved in an angry argument with McCabe in the street and that he entered his house and re-emerged carrying a cleaver, with which he struck McCabe several times. She repeated her statements at the Assize trial of Cash on 19 August 1875.

However, Cash was acquitted of the murder, and it came to light that Maria and two others had been overheard by a witness in a public house concocting the story to ensure Cash's conviction before the coroner's inquest (presumably as the result of a grudge against him). This witness had said nothing at the time as he feared for his life. It transpired that Cash and McCabe had been arguing, but that Cash had been attacked by McCabe's brother with a house-brick and then subjected to a hail of bricks, one of which appears to have struck Winifred McCabe by accident. Maria was found guilty on both counts of perjury and sentenced to seven years' penal servitude on both counts, to run consecutively. The judge stated that 'there was nothing more dangerously affecting human life than perjury in a witness-box'. Her husband seems to have stood by her, and she both sent and received letters throughout her imprisonment.

During her incarceration one of her children, Patrick, died, and her husband wrote to the prison stating 'I am so sorry to say that the information conveyed to my wife, Maria Cain, B204, in reference to the death of our son Patrick is true, he died on 13 February 1876 after a few days' illness, it was not only a fit but of a broken heart after his mother's conviction.' Maria was released on licence in October 1886 and died thirteen years later.

19. Martha Carter (born c.1804, unknown) Licence no. 3790

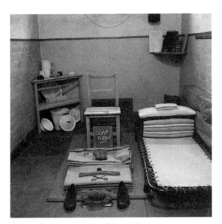

Wakefield Prison cell, 1944
(*Public Domain*)

Wakefield Prison was a local prison, redeveloped to incorporate polygonal and curved wings in 1818. It had a long history before this as a House of Correction from 1594. In the mid-late-nineteenth century the government also rented cells at Wakefield for convicts to undergo separate confinement there. In the 1930s Wakefield was redeveloped as a training prison (see image) and also as a school for prison officers. The prison was designated as part of the 'dispersal' system in 1966. It remains part of the high security estate holding Category A and High Risk Category A prisoners. It also houses a Close Supervision Centre, a small therapeutic unit for the most challenging prisoners.

When Martha Carter was sent to prison in 1864, she was about 60 years old and already had a long criminal career. She was born about 1804 and had committed at least one crime by the time she was thirty, though her criminal career accelerated in her forties. In 1841 she was living with her husband, Dick and their five children in Halifax. In 1844 she was acquitted of a theft at Huddersfield though in 1845 she spent a month in prison for stealing a hat and six months in prison in 1846 for stealing eight quilts. In the next few years she was picked up for larceny, vagrancy, being a 'rogue and vagabond' and spent short periods in prison under local police acts. In January 1851 she was sent to prison for twelve months for stealing a piece of beef. After her release she was again picked up for vagrancy, the newspaper reported her as a common prostitute when she was convicted of being drunk and disorderly. Two months later she was again in court, described as a 'notorious prostitute and thief'; and was found guilty of stealing a sack and fowl and sentenced to ten years' penal servitude at Wakefield Sessions.

After her release on licence in August 1856 she was again convicted of drunkenness in October 1857; in theory she was still under licence, in court, Martha had said that 'she should do better serving out the remainder of her time than knocking about in Huddersfield'. She was sentenced for stealing two glasses from the Rose and Crown in January 1858 and received six years' penal servitude. She went to Millbank and then to Brixton Prison from where she was released on licence in January 1864.

Six months later Martha was back in Wakefield Prison awaiting trial for stealing 14lbs of brown paper. For this offence she was sentenced to ten years' penal servitude and was sent to Millbank and then on to Parkhurst. Fourteen months later she was moved to Brixton. Despite her disorderly life outside prison she does not appear to have committed any offences against the prison rules.

Her husband, Richard, died in 1869 during her imprisonment and at the end of the year she was moved to Woking. Martha was released on licence for a third time in April 1871 with three years and four months of her ten-year sentence remaining. She does not appear to have committed any further crimes. In November 1873, the *Huddersfield Chronicle* reported that three of Martha's sons, Richard, a stonemason, William, a 'fettler' (metalworker) and Thomas, a miner were charged with neglecting to maintain her. The collector for the Board of Guardians said that Martha was chargeable to the Union as she was unable to maintain herself. She had been in Crossland Moor workhouse since 10 September. Her sons did not appear in court. Martha died, two months later, in January 1874.

20. Anthony Castor (born 1896, Lewisham) Licence no. 1465

A cornet (*Authors' Collections*)

Anthony Castor was one of 32 convicts tried in May 1932 for rioting at Dartmoor Prison in January 1932. The riot had been sparked by complaints by the convicts of harsh treatment by prison warders and the poor quality of the food they were being served. Castor was a cook in the prison kitchen and was also a musician in the prison band, being a cornet player. He was asked by a prison warden to blow 'Fall In' (an Army bugle tune) in order to warn the prison warders, which he did, and also (to the laughter of the court) apparently decided to play 'Defaulters' (another Army tune), as he thought it appropriate. 23 prisoners were sentenced to a total of 99 years for their part in the riot.

Anthony Castor's offending career started early; at the age of 12 he was found guilty as the ringleader of a juvenile gang which stole an overcoat valued at five shillings from a schoolboy. He was sentenced to nine strokes of the birch, and at his trial, the *Lancashire Evening Post* of 17 December 1908 stated that 'the father of Castor said his son was practically unmanageable, and had a very bad character. He wished the magistrates to send him away. Only a few weeks ago he stole a suit from the house, and after pawning it made off to Southport'.

His family life was clearly not a happy one, as in July 1909 he was sentenced to three years in Bolton Industrial School, being described as 'beyond the control of his parents', and a month later his father was ordered to contribute two shillings per week to his upkeep at the school. Upon his release he spent a brief time in early 1913 at St Pancras Union Workhouse, under the name of John Thompson.

His father died in 1913, and in the same year, Castor was sentenced at Liverpool Sessions to three years in Borstal on two charges of larceny. On being released from Borstal, Castor served briefly in the 2nd South Lancashire Regiment, before being drummed out of the army and sentenced to six months' hard labour in January 1917 at Liverpool Sessions for stealing £22 and cigarettes at Thornton army camp. Upon his release, he offended almost immediately, being sentenced to twelve months' hard labour at Southend in September 1917 for larceny. A year later, he was sentenced at Clerkenwell, London to three years' penal servitude for burglary.

He was released from Parkhurst Prison on 24 January 1921, but on 5 April his licence was revoked following his larceny of a bicycle at Chester. He was released from Dartmoor Prison on 2 December 1921, but only three months later he was found guilty of manslaughter at the Old Bailey (he had strangled a woman with a silk stocking in an argument over a broken light-fitting). He was released on a second licence on 17 May 1928, but almost immediately re-offended, being sentenced to five years' penal servitude for burglary at Reigate, being found in a woman's bedroom.

He served most of his sentence at Dartmoor Prison, where he was one of the thirty-two individuals charged with rioting at the prison on 24 January 1932. The riot started in the prisoners' exercise yard, and resulted in the administration block being badly damaged by fire and several prison warders being quite seriously injured. The Plymouth police were drafted in to restore order, but were unable to prevent Colonel Turner (the Assistant Prison Commissioner, who had been visiting the prison at the time of the riot) from being struck in the face and (rather ironically) being covered with porridge. Castor appears to have behaved reasonably honourably during the riot, assisting the prison warders and was eventually cleared on all charges. He subsequently disappears from record.

21. Ann Coyne (born c.1845, unknown) Licence no. 94320/7525

Brixton convict nursery (*H. Mayhew and J. Binny*, The Criminal Prisons of London and Scenes of London Life, *1862*)

A nursery existed at Brixton Convict Prison for a short time but after this all babies born in prison were born in local prisons. If a prisoner was pregnant, they remained in the local prison until a certain period after the birth. Usually this was a period during which they might be breastfeeding the baby. When the prisoner went to a convict prison, the child was removed to the care of family or friends or to the workhouse. Mothers in prison went to great lengths to locate their young children and they were permitted 'special letters' in circumstances concerning their children. Some children were adopted and contact was prohibited, unfortunately, others died during their mother's incarceration.

Ann Coyne had a long prison record and her offending had begun in her teens. She was convicted under various aliases, Ann Kelly, Coyle, Gibson, Gill, Devitt; it is possible that some of these aliases are derived from her adoption of the surname of the male partner that she was living with at the time. By 1882 she had already served three sentences of penal servitude as well as serving three short prison sentences and having six other summary convictions. Ann had been born in Liverpool, she was Roman Catholic, had good health and earned her living hawking.

In May 1861 Ann was given a three-year penal servitude sentence for stealing two coats; she went to Millbank, then Brixton and on to Parkhurst Prisons and was released on licence in February 1864. In December 1864 she served a further twelve months for stealing another coat. In 1866 she received a seven-year sentence for stealing three shirts at the October Sessions in Liverpool. She went to Millbank from Liverpool Prison and then onto Parkhurst. After committing only two prison offences during her first sentence, she committed a further eight offences during this sentence. After being moved to Woking, she was released on conditional licence to Eagle House Refuge in January 1871. She was permitted to leave the Refuge at the end of July.

Unfortunately, two months later, Ann was back in court, charged with housebreaking and sentenced to ten years' penal servitude and seven years' police supervision. By Christmas, Ann was back in Millbank and after about a year under separate confinement she was moved to Woking. Here she committed more prison offences, about one per year, largely for rudeness, talking, shouting or similar. Ann was permitted to go to East End Refuge on her release but her licence was to be 'at large', so she may have gone for initial support.

In 1881 Ann was living with Thomas Gill in a lodging house in Liverpool. In February 1882 she was convicted again on two counts of larceny and was sentenced to seven years' penal servitude. She was sent from Walton Prison to Millbank but on arrival they discovered that she was pregnant and after a couple of months in the infirmary she was sent back to Walton Prison. A year later, Ann was sent back to Millbank. Ann had given birth at Walton Prison and documents state that Ellen Coyne had been baptised by Father Nugent in the prison in August 1883. Unfortunately the baby had died as death registers for West Derby show an entry for Ellen Coyne, 'aged 0'. Ann was sent on to Fulham Prison where she worked as a cleaner. She was licensed in October 1886, with two years and four months of her sentence not served.

22. Anne Cruise (born c.1838, Prescot, Lancashire) Licence no. 3553

Following the growth of the prison estate from the early 1860s onward, it was recognised that female prisoners released on licence often had few opportunities available to them and consequently drifted back into a cycle of criminality. Consequently, several societies such as the Discharged Female Prisoners Aid Society were created. This society, based at Nine Elms House, Wandsworth, provided a home where they were expected to work for their board and keep. The Matron kept a strict eye on the residents; no intoxicants were allowed, and it was made clear that if residents did not work, they would be expelled from the home. The *London Daily News* of 25 July 1870 reported that such societies were helping the '4,000 ticket of leave females' overcome such difficulties.

Destitute woman and baby, 1877
(*Authors' Collections*)

At the age of 18 Anne made her first appearance at Kirkdale Magistrates' Court, where she was found guilty of obtaining four pairs of boots by deception. She was sentenced to four months' imprisonment. On 11 December 1860 she was sentenced to four years' penal servitude at Liverpool Assizes for burglary. She may have appeared before the court on previous unrecorded occasions, as she is described as 'an incorrigible rogue'. She pleaded guilty on two charges and was sent to Kirkdale Prison. Anne was transferred to Millbank Prison on 10 January 1861, before being transferred to Brixton Prison on 26 March 1861.

Her behaviour whilst at Brixton suggested that she did not take kindly to receiving instruction; she was insolent to prison guards and fought with other inmates. She appears to have had a relationship with an unnamed man just before she was sent to prison, as a letter from the governor of Brixton Prison states 'the prisoner Ann Cruise, who was referred to you today on account of her violent behaviour in this prison, has an infant of about eighteen months. It is necessary that this woman's child should be kept in the infirmary as it is in very delicate health – its state of health is mostly consequent I believe on ill treatment and neglect on the art of the mother. The prisoner's conduct is such as renders her totally unfit for this prison, and as the child is not separated from her, I beg leave to consider her for removal to Millbank and also to ask if the child may at present remain here under treatment in the infirmary'. She clearly had problems in relating to her child, and a note written on the letter stated that her child was subsequently to remain at Brixton with another prisoner.

Anne was clearly a disturbed individual; a report dated 19 February 1863 states that she should be considered for special removal from Brixton to Fulham 'using fearful and threatening language disturbing the infirmary and frightening the patients, also for repeatedly refusing to give her child the food ordered by the doctor and throwing her own dinner out of the infirmary window and demanding to leave the infirmary contrary to the orders of Doctor Rendle'. In the event she was transferred not to Fulham Prison, but to Millbank, which was noted for its harsh regime. She seems to have served her full sentence, being released in 1864. However, on 17 January 1865 she was sentenced at Lancaster Sessions to seven years' penal servitude for embezzlement as a servant. Her bad behaviour in prison continued throughout her sentence. Despite this, Anne was still released on licence with eighteen months of her sentence 'unserved'. She was sent to the Discharged Female Prisoners' Aid Society at Wandsworth, but then disappears from all records.

23. Harriet Curtis (born 1839, Walsall, Staffordshire) Licence no. 3610

WIFE John! Where is the rest of your wages? How am I going to pay the landlord, and buy food for the children?
HUSBAND Shut up! What I do with my money is no business of yours.

Victorian domestic violence (The Vote, *1911*)

Domestic violence did not often feature as an offence heard at courts in Victorian Britain. Battered spouses were often too frightened of the consequences to report it to the police (who often regarded it as a private matter anyway). Divorce was extremely difficult to obtain, and even if this was achieved, until 1873 custody of any children more often than not went to the husband. Women also had to prove an aggravating factor as well as adultery by their husbands. It was not until the 1873 Married Women (Maintenance in Case of Desertion) Act that women could claim maintenance from their husbands who had wilfully neglected them, and it was not until the 1923 Matrimonial Causes Act that men and women could divorce on equal terms.

Harriet Curtis née Longmore was the daughter of a spur plater – this was a common trade in Walsall, which was the centre of the leather-saddle and harness-making trade in England. Harriet followed her father into the same industry; in the 1861 census she is listed as still living with her parents, being employed as a 'harness furniture-stitcher'. Her dexterity with a sharp instrument was soon to be put to another use.

At the age of 26 in 1866 she married a chandelier maker, Thomas Curtis, at nearby West Bromwich. The marriage was not to prove a happy one. Harriet soon fell pregnant, and gave birth to a son the following year, but unfortunately he died in the winter of that year. This tragedy helped sour the marriage, and on 13 May 1868 Harriet and Thomas agreed to separate (divorce would have been out of the question at the time). On the following day Thomas came back from work and went to see his solicitor. He arrived back home at 11pm and not a word passed between them. The *Birmingham Daily Post* (13 July 1868) stated that 'early next morning he was awoke by smarting sharp pains in his abdomen, and he found his wife was standing over him, cutting and wounding him in his private parts with a razor'. She threatened to dismember him, so he cried 'Murder!', put his trousers on and ran to the nearby General Hospital. He lost a large quantity of blood.

In her defence, Harriet argued that Thomas had infected both her and their dead child with an infectious disease – he hotly contested this, stating that the child had died from consumption. He did however admit that he had on one occasion 'transmitted a loathsome disease to her', and that he had been with other women. His brother, George Curtis, appeared as a witness, and there was clearly little fraternal feeling; he stated that he had seen Thomas beat Harriet on more than one occasion and that he had given her two black eyes.

The jury found Harriet guilty of wounding with intent to cause grievous bodily harm, but recommended her to mercy. The judge was obviously equally sympathetic to her case – he stated that 'there could be no doubt that her husband had behaved very badly towards her', but he could not punish him. He also explained that he had taken account of the jury's recommendation and only sentenced her to five years' penal servitude.

Harriet then unsuccessfully asked if she could claim maintenance from Thomas after she had served her sentence, as he had 'by his treatment and conduct, reduced her to such a state of health as that it would be impossible for her to earn a livelihood by her own industry'. Harriet was released early on orders of the Home Secretary and returned to Walsall in 1871. No further trace of her can be found.

24. Elizabeth Dillon (born 1842, Birmingham) Licence no. A46798/7622

Many petty offenders were picked up on charges of drunkenness and those whose lives revolved around the street, the public house and the prison were easy pickings for the newly established police service. Drink was seen as a precursor of crime and violence. Whilst drink had been seen as a problem at various points in history, the late-nineteenth century viewed habitual drunkenness as a particularly problematic. As prosecutions increased through the 1860s and 1870s drunkenness was increasingly medicalised as inebriety and legislation allowed for those with multiple convictions or who had committed serious offences under the influence of drink to be incarcerated in specific inebriate reformatories.

Elizabeth Dillon, aged 39
(*The National Archives*)

Elizabeth Dillon (alias Lamb) was typical of the majority of female offenders, the offences she committed were petty, though in her case there were lots of them. Elizabeth was born in Birmingham in 1842; she spent her early life with her parents and siblings at Smallbrook Street Court and worked as a pin-header (Birmingham was known at the time as the 'city of a thousand trades', many of them involving small-scale metalwork such as pins).

Ten years later, she was lodging at 42 Vale Street, was single and working as a button maker. Aged 19, she committed two minor offences: riotous and indecent conduct and vagrancy; and was given a four-day prison sentence for each offence. Unfortunately these offences set a tone for the next two decades as Elizabeth committed between one and three offences nearly every year from then on. Often this was for riotous conduct and indecency, but also assault, drunk and disorderly and theft; and she frequently served short prison sentences of between four days and three months, depending on the offence.

In the late 1860s, she was found guilty of aggravated assault, received a two-month prison sentence and later served a further four days for obstruction. In the early 1870s she was imprisoned for streetwalking and as a disorderly prostitute; and for the next thirteen years she continues to appear in court for drunk and riotous behaviour as well as obscene language, assault and fighting. In 1884, she pleaded guilty to stealing two pairs of trousers at the Quarter Sessions; her thirty-four previous convictions were noted by the *Birmingham Daily Post* and reported that the court said though 'a small theft in itself, it was impossible for him to do anything else than send her to penal servitude for five years'.

After an initial period in Birmingham prison, Elizabeth was moved to Millbank Prison where she spent seven months in separate confinement. She was assessed as incapable of work, due to paralysis on her left side and neuralgia and was moved to Woking Prison, where she spent the next thirty-four months. Despite Elizabeth's disorderly behaviour on the city streets, she was the model prisoner, as she did not commit any offences against prison rules. She wrote regularly to her sister Margaret Nicholls and through her to George Dillon, her son, who was residing with her sister due to her imprisonment.

Elizabeth was released on licence with one-third of her sentence remaining, giving her sister's address as her intended place of abode. By 1891, Elizabeth was hawking fish and residing in Birmingham workhouse. Two years later, the *Birmingham Daily Post*, reported that Elizabeth was charged with breaking twelve panes of glass after an altercation with Maria Smith and was carried from the dock screaming at the complainant. By this time she had fifty-four previous convictions. She was back in the district workhouse in 1901 and died in 1906.

25. Julia Donovan (born 1823 Cork, Ireland) Licence no. 7466

Bristol Bridewell Bridge (*Authors' Collections*)

Bristol Bridewell and Common Prison was built in 1820. The prison was condemned in 1873 and Julia would have been one of the last prisoners held there before the prison was demolished. Bristol Prison was built between 1881 and 1883 (although the Georgian frontage with radial-style prison wings behind it was not finally completed until 1889). When Julia returned to Bristol Prison in 1889, she became one of the two hundred prisoners the prison was designed to hold. HMP Bristol today holds three times that number, and is a Category 'B' prison, which also contains a young offender unit.

In the mid–1850s Julia and her husband Patrick moved from Ireland to Bristol. Julia worked for rag-gatherers until 1870 when she was convicted stealing at Bristol and imprisoned for one month. When released from prison she established her own rag-gathering route, but, and this was an occupational hazard of this industry, she was convicted of stealing a shirt in 1871 (six weeks' custody), and a petticoat (six months' custody).

In August 1873, 'Julia Donovan was charged with having a velvet jacket and an earthenware teapot in her possession supposed to have been stolen… on hearing that she had been three times convicted of felony … committed her for trial at the Assizes'. She received a twelve-month sentence. When she stole a towel shortly after her release, her perceived status as a habitual offender ensured a lengthy sentence. At Bristol Assizes she was sent to penal servitude for seven years and five years' police supervision.

Of the eight children she had borne thus far, the three surviving ones lived with their father whilst Julia was in prison. She must have been glad to return to them when she was released on licence in 1879. However, her stay there was fairly short as she was re-convicted of stealing clothes in 1880 and sent back to penal servitude for eight years, followed by five years' police supervision. During that sentence her husband died, and her two sons, Patrick and John, joined the army (being in barracks close to the prison). Her daughter, Mary, was married in 1883 and it was with her and her husband John that she lived when she was released on licence in 1886, with twenty months left unserved.

In 1888 the newspaper reported that 'Julia Donovan, an elderly woman, was charged with stealing a pair of stockings ... the woman was a very old offender and His Lordship said the prisoner had been sentenced to various terms of imprisonment for petty larcenies, and she had served two terms of penal servitude ... these sentences were unjust and absurd, and ought never to have been passed. He should pass a sentence of one day's imprisonment, so that she might be discharged'. She was, but was then convicted just two months later for a similar offence and this time she served another twelve-month sentence.

The census records that when she was released, both Julia (and one of her sons) lived in Bristol Workhouse, and there she stayed until she died in 1909 aged 84. The legacy of poverty and institutional care continued, with 14-year-old John Murphy, Julia's grandson, also being in care with Bristol Union 'Home for Boys'.

26. Margaret Donovan (born c.1853, Holborn, London) Licence no. A44410/504

Coldbath Fields House of Correction
(*Authors' Collections*)

Margaret's partner (both in life and crime), Joseph Christy, was being held in Coldbath Fields Prison at the time of their trial for counterfeiting. Originally built during the reign of James I, the prison in which Christy found himself was constructed as the Middlesex House of Correction in 1794, designed to hold rogues and vagabonds rather than convicts. In 1810 former Bow Street Runner William Adkins, was elected as its Governor, and he was succeeded in 1823 by another former Runner, John Vickery. By the 1850s, the prison had expanded, with almost 1450 prisoners being detained there. By the time of Margaret and Joseph's offence, the prison was also used as a short-term holding place for suspects awaiting trial.

Little is known of the first thirty years of Margaret Donovan's life, apart from her approximate year of birth and her birthplace. However, in 1884, she appears at the Central Criminal Court (Old Bailey) alongside her partner, Joseph Christy, on a charge of feloniously manufacturing counterfeit coin. The *Standard* of 18 January reported that two police officers had raided their home at 55 Wentworth Street in Whitechapel and that they 'found the two prisoners sitting at a table, on which where were spread a number of counterfeit coins, and the prisoners there engaged in filing other coins'. It appears that the two defendants had been caught red-handed manufacturing false florins (two-shilling pieces).

Both defendants pleaded not guilty at their trial, but were both found guilty; Christy was sentenced to seven years' penal servitude, whilst Margaret received a sentence of five years' penal servitude. The authorities at Millbank Prison sent out letters enquiring about Margaret's character and background in March 1884, and received a reply from CID at Scotland Yard, stating that information on her went back ten years, but that nothing was known 'against her character previous to the present charge excepting that she associated with low characters and was addicted to drink'.

Her character with regard to industry was described as 'indifferent', whilst her sobriety was described as 'bad'. She had no known means of livelihood, and was co-habiting with Christy (to whom she had claimed to be married), and that she was in fact a widow and her real surname was Ready. Her class and habits of life were described as 'very low', as were the characters of her friends and associates.

This damning report appears to be the reason as to why on 18 April 1884 an order was given that she was not to be placed in Star Class (the class usually assigned to first-time offenders such as Margaret). This would have meant a harder life in prison for Margaret, but she managed to serve her time without causing any problems for the authorities. She was visited by her father, brother and son whilst in prison and kept up a regular correspondence with her married sister. She was released on conditional licence to the East End Refuge with 28 months not served on her sentence on 28 August 1886. She continued to be well-behaved and was released on a full licence from the refuge on 28 May 1887.

She does not appear to have offended again, disappearing from the criminal records. The 1891 census records a Margaret Ready as a widowed laundress living in the East End with two children. This may well be Margaret Donovan; if so it is the last we can find of her; her post-offending life, like her pre-offending life, remains a mystery.

27. Mary Ann Dougherty (born 1832, Connaught, Ireland) Licence no. 19494/7607

Parkhurst Prison on the Isle of Wight first opened in 1838 as a separate institution for juvenile offenders. Juvenile offenders, in the end only boys, were housed there to undergo the separate system of imprisonment. From 1863 to 1869 it held female convicts and from then on only male convicts. Parkhurst became part of the high security 'dispersal' system from 1966; dispersing the most dangerous prisoners across the system. It gained much notoriety as a tough prison over the years, but one infamous escape in 1995 lead to its removal from the dispersal system. Parkhurst is now part of a larger prison site, bringing three prisons on the island together under the rubric of HMP Isle of Wight.

Mary Ann Dougherty aged 49 (*Ancestry.com*)

Mary Ann Dougherty was born in Ireland in the 1830s, but the family moved to Leeds, as at the age of 20 she was working as a house servant and living with her widowed mother and siblings at Allison's Buildings. In her twenties she was convicted of ten summary offences for which she spent short periods in Leeds Prison.

In 1866, Mary was convicted of stealing money from the person and sentenced to seven years' penal servitude by Wakefield Sessions. Her conduct in Wakefield Prison had been very bad though it improved after she was moved to Millbank Prison. In July 1866 she was moved to Parkhurst where she worked in association at needlework. She also committed fourteen prison offences after she was moved to Woking in April 1869. Mary got into trouble for rudeness, quarrelling, fighting, singing, causing a disturbance and was punished by periods of close confinement, losing class or remission marks and once was restrained in a straitjacket. In July 1870, Mary received a conditional licence to Eagle House Refuge.

Unfortunately, Mary was not out of prison for long as she breached the conditions of her licence after being sentenced to three months at Wakefield as a 'rogue and a vagabond' in May 1871. She was sent back to Millbank. Mary petitioned for her licence to be renewed, claiming she had regularly reported herself to the police, she had found a good situation and would have remained there; but the Lady Superior of the Roman Catholic Refuge had informed her employer that she had been a convict. Her petition was refused. In July 1872 she was moved to Woking Prison. She committed a further four prison offences, her sentence expired in March 1874 and she was released.

In 1878, Mary spent some time in Middlesex Lunatic Asylum though she was discharged in May. She committed two further thefts and then in January 1881 she was sentenced to seven years' penal servitude by Hull Sessions for stealing a watch from the person. In February she was sent from Hull Prison back to Millbank and in July to Woking. She remained there until her release on licence in October 1885.

Mary committed another six prison offences and evidence suggests she felt the police were constantly watching her, though the Superintendent of Middlesex Asylum thought she feigned insanity. She was described as weak-minded, she continued to be disruptive, feeling frustrated and unjustly treated. She was released again on licence in October 1885 but this was also revoked as she failed to report herself to Hull police within 48 hours. She received a special licence in March 1887 when she was about 55 years old and intended to go to Mark Dougherty in Leeds, possibly her brother or son.

28. Thomas Douglas (born 1841, Distington, Cumbria) Licence no. 43524/ 22486

Broadmoor Asylum c. 1867 (*Public Domain*)

Designed by Lt Col. Joshua Jebb, Broadmoor Criminal Lunatic Asylum admitted its first patient (a woman convicted of infanticide) on 27 May 1863. The first male patients arrived on 27 February 1864. Thomas Douglas was therefore one of the first males to experience the secure regime at the Hospital. Never part of the prison system, the high walls and barbed wire were still designed to separate out those who were deemed dangerous in order that they could receive treatment. Whilst Thomas was in Broadmoor it was still under construction, being completed only in 1868. Still in use today, it has held men such as Ronnie Kray and Peter Sutcliffe (the "Yorkshire Ripper").

As a young man, Thomas enlisted as a Private in the 2nd Battalion 4th Regiment of Foot. Described on his prison record as a soldier or sailor, and given the 'anchor' tattoo on his right arm, it is likely he was one of the marines in the King's Own Regiment (later the Royal Lancashire Regiment) who would have fought in the Abyssinian campaign of 1868 if he had not been dismissed from the service in 1860. The 19-year old Private struck his superior officer and was court martialled whilst his regiment was stationed in Corfu.

Back home in the UK, he was sent to Millbank to start his ten years' penal servitude. He didn't take easily to prison life and was frequently in trouble for laughing and talking in church, exchanging library books for bread with other prisoners, breaking windows, refusing to work, and, in 1861, striking a prison warder. For striking a 'severe blow' at the warder he received twenty-eight days' bread and water diet and lost sixty days' remission. Six months later he was further punished for conspiring with other prisoners to attack the warder again.

The young man was clearly troubled, and he was sent to Fisherton Lunatic Asylum for four months in 1863, before returning to Dartmoor Prison. There he assaulted an officer on the works by throwing a stone and striking him on the forehead and then striking him in the face with another stone whilst he was on the ground. He was sent to Broadmoor Hospital in September 1864.

There is no mention in the licence folder that during his time at Broadmoor, Douglas made several escape attempts, one of them partially successful. He tried to escape with three other inmates in December 1864, and finally managed it on his second attempt on 9 November 1868. He originally struck out south, walking from South Berkshire to Southampton where, as a former sailor, he hoped to get a boat passage to America. He was unsuccessful in this, so turned north and finally gave himself up starving and exhausted in Lancaster on 30 November 1868.

Perhaps he was attempting to find his old regiment? In any case, after this experience he was then apparently a changed man, biddable and cooperative – he worked in the garden at Broadmoor and asked to be returned to prison (which he was in 1870). He only spent one month in Millbank, however, before he was released on one month's early release licence. He returned to Cumbria, the place of his birth, but was re-convicted in 1881 at Portsmouth for assaulting a police officer.

His problem with authority combined with his mental illnesses caused him to return to Broadmoor, where he saw out his life. Thomas died of heart disease at the age of 62, in Broadmoor, in 1903.

29. Catherine Doyle (born 1851, Manchester) Licence no. 55581/7566

BIRD'S-EYE VIEW OF MILLBANK PRISON.
(Copied from a Model by the Clerk of the Works.)

Millbank Prison (*H. Mayhew and J. Binny,*
The Criminal Prisons of London and Scenes
of London Life, *1862*)

Millbank Prison opened in 1816. Convicts thought capable of reform were imprisoned in this fortress on the side of the River Thames for up to ten years rather than being transported. Construction of the prison was problematic due to marshy ground, and epidemics swept through the prison in the 1820s because of the poor ventilation. It was also an expensive institution to run. When Pentonville took over as national penitentiary in 1842, Millbank then held convicts in solitary confinement prior to transportation. Millbank finally closed in 1890.

In 1868, Catherine spent seven days in prison for stealing a jacket, and another six months for stealing a cloak. She was a 16-year-old girl, height four feet-nine inches, of dark complexion, with brown hair, dark grey eyes, cuts on the centre and left of forehead, pockmarked face, a mole near the front of mouth, and her ears were pierced. She was Roman Catholic, single, and living with her mother, a factory worker, in Manchester.

The following year she was imprisoned again for theft of a jacket, and her record noted the addition of a blue mark on the fourth finger of her left hand. This was usually a personal record of the number of times someone had been in prison, although it is not always a reliable index. She was released in July 1870, and was back inside in August for stealing boots. At the age of 18, and now a mother, she received her first penal servitude for stealing wool. Seven years' custody would be followed by seven years' police supervision.

She served her first few months in separate confinement (as all new prisoners did) at Millbank and then Fulham Prison. She made good progress at her schoolwork, and worked well at her knitting duties. Thereafter she was often in trouble. She was punished with a reduced diet and restrained in a straitjacket for destroying prison property and general disorder: ' … returning from chapel in the afternoon by walking up the staircase arm in arm with prison 1031 Mary Wallace, laughing talking loudly and shouting at 4.30pm'; 'singing, shouting and creating a great disturbance in the Hall at 12.30pm'.

In 1877 she was discharged to Fulham Female Refuge, and then released on licence, with two-and-a-half years left to serve on her sentence. She immediately married Francis Doyle, a respectable working man, and in a couple of years they had three children living with the young couple. This seems to have stabilised Catherine, and she did not re-offend until 1882 when she received seven years' penal servitude and seven years police supervision for theft of cloth in Manchester.

On this sentence, her behaviour in prison was much worse, with frequent breaches of prison rules. The worst was in February when she was brought up 'for shouting and kicking violently at her cell door, resisting the male officer, causing a disturbance in the hall, during the silence of the tea half hour, for suddenly rushing out of the corridor across the exercise yard, violently resisting the male officer, striking him a blow on the face, using threatening language towards him and saying that she would pay him out [seriously assault him] even if she had to do seven years.'

On her early release in 1887, she was considered for emigration to America, but she stayed in England with her husband and children, never re-offended again, and died in the early 1900s shortly before her husband.

30. **William Dunnage** (born 1800, Bishops Stortford, Hertfordshire) Licence no. 271

Bow Street Magistrates' Court, 1808
(*Authors' Collections*)

The Bow Street Runners were founded in the winter of 1748/9 by Henry Fielding, the famous novelist, who was also Chief Magistrate of Bow Street, Westminster from 1748-54. They were the world's first detective force, and operated throughout both London and the rest of Great Britain. They never wore any form of uniform, always operating in plain clothes, and their only badge of office was a small baton called a tipstaff. They were small in number, and were disbanded in 1839, but had a considerable influence on the creation of later detective forces such as C.I.D. and Scotland Yard.

William Dunnage did not trouble the courts until 1825, when on 14 July he was convicted with Charles Searle at Hertfordshire Assizes for stealing rabbits. They were both sentenced to be transported for seven years. This appears at first sight to be a fairly mundane offence and sentence, but it was connected to other events that were to have consequences for the inhabitants of Bishops Stortford.

In March and April a number of arson offences were perpetrated in the town; the White Horse public house was attacked on two occasions, whilst the premises of a Mr Francis, a draper, were also torched. Following the arrest of Dunnage and Searle on the charge of rabbit-stealing, a number of anonymous threatening letters were sent, including one that attempted to tie in their release with the arson attacks; it stated: 'To the committee at the vestry [this referred to the parish council which had issued a reward of £500 for the capture of the arsonist], Revenge is sweet: we defy your police or your £500. We are strong, you are weak. If Searle and Dunnage do not come home, Stortford shall be laid in ashes. I am their captain and leader, and we are sworn to revenge. I alone am possessed of a secret to fire any premises at one hundred yards distance. So watch on. There are three of your committee who have made themselves very busy on this occasion, whom we have sworn to send to Paradise as soon as possible'. These events caused consternation in the town and a senior Bow Street Runner, Daniel Bishop, was employed along with a less senior colleague to seek out the offender(s). They conducted their enquiries and suspicion fell upon Thomas Rees, the son of Mr Francis' neighbour. He was tried in July 1825 at Hertfordshire Assizes, and though he was found not guilty of the actual arson attacks, he was found guilty of sending at least one threatening letter; and subsequently transported for life.

Dunnage himself, although sentenced to be transported, actually served his sentence on the prison hulk *Ganymede*, moored at Chatham. He received a pardon just over four years into his sentence and returned to Bishops Stortford. He does not appear to have learned much from this confinement, and twenty-three years later he found himself back in court at Hertfordshire Assizes, charged with stealing a sheep. He was found guilty and sentenced to ten years' transportation. Again, he was not actually transported, this time spending much of his sentence on the *Stirling Castle* invalid prison hulk (suggesting that he did not enjoy good health).

He was released on licence after serving just under six years of his sentence, and again returned to his family at Bishops Stortford. In July 1867 a William Dunnage was found guilty of burglary after a previous conviction of felony at Hertfordshire Assizes and sentenced to eight months' imprisonment, suggesting that this was the same individual, despite his being 67 years old at the time. He died in Bishops Stortford in the spring of 1870.

31. **William Edward Eicke** (born c.1829, Blackheath, Kent) Licence no. 81

An Old Bailey courtroom (*Authors' Collections*)

The Old Bailey originated as the sessions house of the Lord Mayor and Sheriffs of the City of London and Middlesex in the sixteenth century. After rebuilding it emerged as a major court dealing with London's serious offenders in the eighteenth century. In 1834, it was renamed the Central Criminal Court, and its jurisdiction was extended from the mid-nineteenth century to take in serious offences committed throughout England and Wales. So, although Eicke was dealt with as a local man in 1851, by 1856 notorious offenders from further afield were also pleading their case in the Old Bailey. The present court building opened in 1907. Above the main entrance is inscribed 'Defend the Children of the Poor & Punish the Wrongdoer', and watching over the court's activities is a bronze statue entitled 'Lady Justice'.

Man of Kent, William Edward Eicke was taller than most convicts at over six feet tall. He was also one of the few men who found themselves in convict prison that had enjoyed a good career before experiencing the darker side of life. He had been a clerk in the office of the Treasurer to the London and South West Railway Company (for a number of years up to 1850), and thereafter a chemist (1851 census) before he was convicted of 'larceny as a servant', after being found guilty of stealing a debenture bond worth £2,000 from his employer at London's Central Criminal Court in 1851.

His father was a solicitor and the family could afford a barrister to represent William, but all to no avail, as he was sentenced to seven years' penal servitude; and sent to wait on the prison hulk *Defence* until a transport ship would take him to Australia. As convict transportation as a system of punishment was beginning to wind down in this period he never actually sailed south, but was released on licence with approximately four years of his sentence left to serve.

William almost immediately married Eliza Tappin, a sweetheart who may have waited for him whilst he served his time perhaps? In any case, marriage, and the support of his family must have been significant in him re-establishing his life. The couple moved to Marylebone, and although he is described as a man living on independent means in the 1861 census, the 1871 census has him working as an auctioneer. He stayed in that occupation until 1891, but soon after that date his wife Eliza died, and in 1896 he remarried. His second marriage, to Clara, also saw him change his job to become a commercial agent, living in the Edgeware Road, Paddington.

Whether they simply got fed up of living in London, or whether a new opportunity presented itself, William and Clara underwent significant life-changes in their later lives. In his 70s, he became landlord of the George and Dragon public house in Princes Risborough, Buckinghamshire. Potentially a quieter and more pleasant place to see out his life, he remained there for a couple of years until he died in 1906. He was survived by his wife Clara and left £262 in his will.

Looking back, the early release of William seemed to have been justified. Not only did he never re-offend, but he also managed to make a successful life for himself and for each of his two wives. We will never know whether his family came to be reconciled with William's one fateful interaction with the criminal justice system, or whether William would have had a different life had he never offended, never been caught, or actually been transported to Australia.

32. **Dryden Elstob** (born 1824, London) Licence no. 483

King's Dragoon Guard
(*Authors' Collections*)

Desertion was commonplace (especially during times of conflict) and branding with a hot iron was introduced as a counter-measure during the English Civil War. By 1800 branding had been replaced with a type of tattooing of the letter 'D' – a question in the House of Commons elicited the following statement in 1847: "The House would see that it was absolutely necessary that some means should exist by which a man practising desertion should be known again; and no other means had been discovered, especially since the lash had been discouraged, but that of marking the man with the letter 'D', which was nothing more than a kind of tattooing, which sailors voluntarily underwent. The deserter was tattooed with the letter 'D' by the point of a needle fixed in cork."

Dryden's mother Elizabeth died shortly after the birth of Dryden's younger sister and his father (also Dryden) remarried in 1830. This seems to have affected the younger Dryden adversely – many years later he reportedly stated that 'he had a stepmother and there were family differences'. Dryden senior appears to have been a frequent bankrupt, but he continued to bounce back, and is listed as a Director of the Argus Life Assurance Company of London.

In the 1841 census the younger Dryden is listed as a naval cadet. The navy life does not appear to have suited him however, and in 1843 he enlisted in the 3rd Dragoon Guards. Posted to Ireland, Dryden soon tired of this life as well, and he deserted. He was tried and imprisoned, but subsequently escaped. He was recaptured but then escaped again whilst awaiting a second trial and fled to London. Recognised after six months on the run, he was taken before Bow Street Magistrates' Court and tried and imprisoned for two years. He was also tattooed as a deserter. Dryden feigned insanity shortly after his trial and escaped yet again (earning the sobriquet 'Cavalry Jack Sheppard' after the famous eighteenth-century serial gaol-breaker). He was recaptured and served a year in Cork City Prison, before being transferred to Scotland, where he was to rejoin his regiment after serving the remainder of his sentence. He escaped yet again, but was recognised (although dressed in naval uniform at the time) by a police officer in London who had previously served in the same regiment.

After serving his sentence, Dryden was released, but in 1848 was sentenced at Nottingham Barracks General Court Martial to six months' imprisonment for larceny and seven years' transportation for yet again deserting his regiment. The sentence of transportation was commuted to penal servitude, and on 2 March 1854 he was released on licence from Pentonville Prison.

Dryden Elstob's subsequent life was just as interesting. He appeared at the Insolvent Debtors' Court in June 1857, having tried his hand at farming in Suffolk, Surrey and Hertfordshire. The *Essex Standard* (26 June 1857) reported that he 'was in the habit of getting drunk and driving around to the annoyance of other people', whilst the *Morning Post* (2 February 1858) reported that at his trial for the larceny of a coat, he stated that 'he had tried to get into debt as much as he could and never intended paying another farthing that he could avoid'. In February 1860 he was sentenced at the Old Bailey to another eighteen months' imprisonment for fraud. The last we hear of the intrepid Dryden junior is in September 1864, when a Dryden Elstob of King's Road, Chelsea, described as a 'boarding-house keeper' was declared bankrupt.

33. Jane Field (born 1828, Barnet, Hertfordshire) Licence no. 7478

Tothill Fields Prison exercise yard (*H. Mayhew and J. Binny*, The Criminal Prisons of London and Scenes of London Life, *1862*)

Tothill Fields Prison had a previous incarnation as the Middlesex or Westminster Gaol. In 1834 the House of Correction re-opened as a prison for women and male prisoners aged under 17 years old. The shamrock-shaped prison held approximately 300 prisoners in each of its three wings; the centre comprising exercise yards, as can be seen in the illustration opposite (which shows female prisoners and their children). The main entrance in Francis Street showed the public face of the prison with its massive blocks of granite and large iron gates. The site underwent yet another transformation when the land was obtained in order to build an extension to Westminster Roman Catholic Cathedral (opened in 1903).

None of the four offences Jane committed between 1856 and 1858 (offences which earned her nearly two years in a local prison) were reported in the London newspapers. Her trial at the Old Bailey for theft in 1860, however, did receive much more attention, and opprobrium: 'An impudent prostitute, named Jane Field, whose effrontery stood by her to the last, was sentenced to three years' penal servitude for robbing a man of his watch.'

Jane was a married woman at this time, although she was also recorded as a widow too, so maybe she was estranged from her husband, and had turned to prostitution or theft in order to survive. She served her time, but was then re-convicted in 1863; and this time she received a six-year sentence. She started off in Westminster (or Tothill Fields Prison), and was then transferred to Millbank and Brixton convict prisons. This was the first time that she had complained of ill-health, although throughout her many prison sentences her medical condition was not considered serious by the prison medical officers. For example, she was disciplined for refusing to leave her bed one morning when ordered to do so by the Medical Officer in 1868.

In February 1870, Jane was released from prison, but was back at Tothill Fields in 1871 when she started to serve a seven-year sentence for robbery from the person. The following year she was committed to a hospital bed in Woking Prison, and between December 1872 and September 1876 Jane was in the Woking Prison Infirmary thirteen times, suffering from epilepsy. In November 1876 she was released on licence, but, as previously, she quickly re-offended and was sentenced to ten years' penal servitude at Surrey Quarter Sessions for 'Larceny from the Person (described in the newspapers as 'a shocking robbery committed by women')'.

On this sentence, she was again subject to many epileptic episodes, and she was confined to the Infirmary very frequently. On one occasion she received treatment for a 'trifling' injury she suffered during one of her fits. As was quite commonplace in prisons in this period, the prison authorities treated her condition as a minor one, and they did not consider her epilepsy to merit any special dispensation or reduction in prison workload. As the Medical Officer stated in 1882, 'she is subject to epileptic fits of a mild form. Her general health is good and it is uninjured by her imprisonment.' On 16 July 1886, Jane was released on licence fourteen months early. Aged in her 60s, she then appears to have stopped offending, and she never reappears in criminal justice records.

34. Margaret Fitzmorris (born 1855, Manchester) Licence no. A46179/ 7583

Prisoners being released from gaol (*H. Mayhew and J. Binny*, The Criminal Prisons of London and Scenes of London Life, *1862*)

Since the 1860s there were attempts to keep a watchful eye over released convicts, at least for the period they were released on licence. The 1869 Habitual Offender Act and the Prevention of Crime Act (1871) extended this power by giving the sentencing Judge the power to order a set period of police supervision for persistent offenders. On release from prison, supervisees were required to report to the police, inform them every fortnight of where they were residing. If any person under supervision re-offended, consorted with thieves and prostitutes, or could not prove they were making an honest living, they could be imprisoned for up to a year. Police supervision was finally abandoned in the 1930s.

Family was important to Margaret, and concerns about her siblings, husband, and children played a part in her offending and prison life. Possibly her early separation from her parents, for some unknown reason, caused her to attach importance to those family members that she could cling on to. She worked alongside her sister, both in their mid-teens, in a Manchester cotton factory and was frequently convicted of drunkenness and street disorders until 1880 (with one conviction under the name of Margaret Cain for larceny of a skirt at Manchester earning her six months in prison in 1875). She was then sentenced to twelve-months' prison for stealing wincey (a light but strong fabric typically made of a mixture of wool with cotton or linen); on release she was charged and acquitted of another theft before being convicted of stealing forty yards of wincey material, the property of Robert Lloyd at Manchester; and receiving five years' penal servitude and three years' police supervision in 1884.

By then she was married and had a child, and throughout her sentence she wrote to them, and also to her sister, as regularly as was allowed. Margaret also attempted to write to her brother, but as he was a ticket-of-leave man that had breached his conditional licence and been returned to prison, he was deemed to be an unsuitable recipient for correspondence. When her sister was also imprisoned in a convict prison she was then not allowed to send letters to her either (although when her sister was sent to the East End Refuge before being finally released, the exchange of letters resumed).

In 1886 Margaret enquired whether the Discharged Prisoners' Aid Society could arrange for her child to attend a Roman Catholic School. Things were clearly not going well at home. A little later she asked the prison authorities why she had not heard from her husband for a year. Her prison file contains a letter from Detective Superintendent Hicks who reported that her child was well and living with Mrs Daley who formerly kept the 'Flowerpot' beer-house, Ancoats Lane, although her present address was unknown. Her husband had travelled into the country about six months ago looking for work and had not yet returned. It must have been with some relief that Margaret received a letter from her husband from a new address in Salford in November 1886.

On 31 January 1887, Margaret was removed to the East End Refuge in Finchley that had held her sister. Two years and four months before her sentence fully expired, the Directors permitted her to leave the refuge on conditional licence on 31 October 1887. In 1890 Margaret was back before the courts, sentenced to twelve months and three years' police supervision for larceny in Manchester. Five years later she was found guilty of shopbreaking and sentenced to six months' imprisonment in Strangeways, with her record stating that she had a total of 23 previous convictions. In 1897 she received five months for larceny, and a further six months in 1899 for stealing. Her offending continued into the twentieth century; in 1901 she received six months for stealing and was sentenced to nine months at Manchester in December 1904 for stealing thirty yards of velveteen. She then disappears from the record. Her affection for her husband, and the possibility of being separated from him and her child yet again may have dissuaded her from future offending, because she was never convicted of another offence.

35. John Fletcher (born 1836, Manchester) Licence no. A20395

Old Moorish Castle, Gibraltar (*Authors'*
Collections)

The Gibraltar Penal Station was established in 1841, and the establishment continued to take in convicts undertaking penal servitude overseas until 1871. The convicts sent there were employed in substantially reinforcing the naval fortifications that made Gibraltar such a strategic stronghold in the First and Second World Wars. The prison was based in the old Moorish Castle. Major Arthur Griffiths, Governor at Gibraltar from 1864 to 1870 later became Deputy-governor of Chatham (1870-2), of Millbank (1872-4), of Wormwood Scrubs (1874-81), and finally he became Inspector of Prisons (1878-96) and an established author of many books on prison history.

John had been in local prisons three times (for theft of money, of chickens, and an aggravated assault) by the time he received his first penal servitude. A married man, he was convicted of two offences (stealing, and receiving stolen property) at Manchester, and received sentences of three and four years' penal servitude to run concurrently. During this sentence he breached prison regulations twenty-seven times. His offences included the usual disorderliness of shouting, talking, and laughing in places and times which were prohibited; breaking prison property; and not completing his work tasks satisfactorily; but he was also guilty of a number of violent offences. He fought with fellow prisoners quite regularly, and he was also aggressive to prison warders. That might explain why he did not receive a ticket-of-leave, and he served his full sentence in Wakefield, Chatham, Portsmouth, and Dartmoor prisons.

He was re-convicted in 1867. This time he received seven years' penal servitude and seven years' supervision at Salford Quarter Sessions for theft. He was imprisoned in Pentonville before being transferred to Gibraltar Penal Station in May 1868, where he remained for four years. It was there that he committed a serious violent offence. His explanation of the event was that he had approached a fellow prisoner who had been spreading rumours about him in prison. 'I went to ask him that morning what he did that for. He said because I deserved it and that I was a swine. I told him to stand up. I had a hammer in my hand. I struck him with my right fist. He fell against a bunker and cut his head and he has put all the prisoners against me.' However, the victim of the assault stated: 'If I would find out who it was [spreading rumours] I would dash their brains in. I said you should not be so rash as that, if you had come and asked, I might have told you. There was some more talk, nothing of any consequence, and then he walked off and said "if you say so" and I said "yes" and then he struck me a blow on the forehead with a hammer and knocked me down – he fell with me. I was stunned for the moment. The next thing I received two blows on my right shoulder as I was lying on the ground. I was bleeding from the blows on my face and neck... Nothing more passed between the prisoner and myself at that time nor at any other time. I never had an angry word with the man in my life.'

For that assault he received fifteen years' penal servitude, which he served in various prisons until his release in 1875. His licence was almost immediately revoked, and he was returned to prison to serve the rest of his sentence, and was ultimately not released until 1887. He was a man who committed offences inside and outside of prison until his death in Manchester in 1898, aged 63.

36. Isabella Fraser (born c.1812, Liverpool) Licence no. A45450/7564

Victorian Liverpool (*Public Domain*)

Isabella had a long criminal career, but only experienced a convict prison late in life. When that happened in 1884, her prison record revealed a long list of previous offences: 'H.M.P. Chester, 21st January 1881 at Birkenhead, stealing wearing apparel, 3 calendar months as Marg. Hutton; 18th August 1873 at Birkenhead, stealing wearing apparel, 3 calendar months as Marg. Fraser; 11th February 1874 at Birkenhead, stealing mutton, 3 calendar months as Marg. McDonald; summarily convicted for drunkenness; Knutsford May Sessions 1876, stealing a coat, 18 calendar months

> Liverpool Workhouse was praised in the 1832 Royal Commission Report for its segregation of the sexes, a long working day, and the almost constant confinement of the inmates. In 1842 the Brownlow Hill site was quickly enlarged to become one of the largest workhouses in the country, holding approximately 3,000 inmates (though the site sometimes held 2,000 more than the official capacity). Fortunately for women like Isabella, she was not yet a resident when the workhouse caught fire in 1862; on 7 September, 21 children and two nurses were burnt to death. The Workhouse was demolished in 1931 to make the site available for the new Catholic Cathedral.

as Marg. McDonough; Liverpool, July Sessions 1872, stealing braces, 4 calendar months as Marg. McDonough; August Sessions 1874, stealing a pewter measure, 12 calendar months, as above; October Sessions 1878, stealing 2½ lbs of butter, 12 calendar months as Isabella Frazer; 3rd August 1882 at Birkenhead, stealing 3 brushes, 6 weeks, as Marg. McDonough; November City Sessions 1882, stealing a box of butterine, 12 calendar months as above. And 41 times summary drunkenness, obscene language and not accounting & etc, sentences 3 days to 2 calendar months.'

With this considerable record under her belt, Isabella was fortunate not to have been sentenced to penal servitude before she did. In fact she had a narrow escape in 1839 when she was acquitted of stealing wearing apparel. Had that conviction been made out, she would have been sent to convict prison aged 25. As it was she then committed more minor offences for the next forty or so years, ones which resulted in her being confined in local prisons for shorter sentences, up to twelve months. When aged 66, however, she was convicted of stealing nine-and-three-quarter lbs of bacon, and given five years' penal servitude at Liverpool.

Isabella is described in her prison record as being a hawker (mobile trader), of sallow complexion, grey hair, grey eyes, just over five feet tall, oval face, stout build; her face very much scarred, right side of neck, both arms and both legs, ears pierced. Her health was indifferent and she suffered from rheumatism, as many prisoners did; and her health had probably not improved by the time of her release on licence in 1887. By this time she was in her 70s, but age did not stop or even slow her re-offending. She was convicted in Liverpool over the next three years following for theft. She alternated between being housed in local prisons, and the Liverpool Workhouse, until she died in the workhouse in 1896. Aged about 80 (for her birth date varies in different records), she had perhaps been fortunate to escape convict prison in her youth and middle ages, but the short prison episodes, together with poverty, and life in the workhouse, must have caused her a great measure of misery over the course of her life.

37. Caroline Goode (born 1836, Walsall) Licence no. 3586

Commutation of sentence is where a guilty person has their sentence reduced after petitioning the government. The prisoner is still guilty; they are not pardoned, but if commutation is allowed then their sentence is reduced. Petitions for commutation of sentence often came from the defendant but they could also come from family, friends and associates on their behalf. Death sentences received in the eighteenth and early nineteenth centuries were often commuted to transportation overseas for life or for long periods. After the end of transportation in the 1860s, when permitted, death sentences were commuted to imprisonment, specifically penal servitude for life or for long periods, depending on the case.

A Victorian Hanging Room
(*Authors' Collections*)

On 15 December 1859 Caroline Goode was sentenced to death at Warwick Assizes for administering poison with the intent to murder. The sentence she received was later commuted to fifteen years' penal servitude. Caroline had been found guilty of feloniously administering laudanum to her infant child, Mary Ann Goode, in Birmingham on 27 October 1859.

Caroline was a servant, who lived on Constitution Hill; she was single and her daughter Mary Ann was nursed by a woman on Milk Street. Caroline had been lodging with Mrs Parry since 15 September and had brought a female infant with her. On 13 October she had gone to work, leaving the child in the charge of Mrs Parry. Caroline regularly saw her child at Mrs Parry's house. It was claimed that on 27 October Caroline had come to the house when Mrs Parry was out and the infant was being fed by her daughter Jane. Mrs Parry returned to find the child asleep and her daughter called her attention to the child's food. She tasted it, finding it bitter and having a disagreeable smell.

She went to the prisoner's house to ask her if she had put anything in the baby's food. Caroline denied that she had and promised to see the child but failed to do so. In the meantime the baby had become ill, swelling up and exhibited a purple tone. The doctor was called and in time the baby recovered. At the trial, Jane Parry stated that the prisoner had asked her to go upstairs and on her return was stirring the baby's food. Jane put the food in the oven to warm and fed the baby with it. Before the infant had eaten half of the food, she fell into a long deep sleep and was breathing heavily. The food was later analysed by Professor Wrightson who stated that it contained about an eighth part of a grain of morphia, though he thought it dangerous to give half that amount to a child. The jury found Caroline guilty and sentenced her to death *(Daily News*, 19 December, 1859), but the sentence was later commuted upon appeal to the Home Secretary to penal servitude for fifteen years.

Caroline spent separate confinement at Millbank and was then moved to Brixton Prison. At Brixton she committed fifteen offences against the prison rules. None of these occurred in the first four years of her imprisonment, but after this she started to get into trouble for insolence, disorderly conduct, refusing to work and destroying prison property. As a result of these offences she lost remission marks, spent time on punishment diet or in close confinement and on one occasion, eighteen hours in handcuffs.

In December 1869 she was transferred to Millbank and then released on licence, four years and six months early. She listed her intended place of abode as her parent's home in Balsall, Warwickshire. Caroline did not commit any further crimes; she did not marry and continued to work in Birmingham as a servant.

38. Ann Gorst (born c.1844, Ireland) Licence no. 7448

Prostitution is not an offence in English law but there are offences related to the practice. Those often labelled as 'prostitutes' were charged with specific offences such as soliciting, living off immoral earnings, or running a house of ill-repute (brothel). Women on the streets were often charged with other offences such as indecency, drunkenness, disorderly conduct which were dealt with summarily and enforced selectively. In the nineteenth century there was considerable concern about prostitution and it was described by *The Times* as 'the greatest of our social evils' and prostitutes were seen as the antithesis to the ideal of respectable Victorian middle-class femininity and womanhood.

Ann Gorst (*The National Archives*)

Ann Gorst (née Ward) was born in Ireland in 1844, probably in Dundalk where her brother still lived, but by the early 1870s she was living in Liverpool. During the 1870s and 1880s she was in court multiple times for prostitution, being an 'incorrigible rogue', or 'suspected person', stealing, drunkenness and assaulting the police. In fact between 1869 and 1883 she accumulated numerous offences and spent short periods in local prisons for these crimes. In 1882 she was also convicted for being drunk and disorderly in Manchester, in Ashton-under-Lyne and in Barrow. In 1883 she was convicted for stealing and another seven times for being drunk in Bury. In 1883 Gorst also returned to Liverpool and spent one month in prison for fighting. In the October of that year she was convicted of stealing one shawl, one basket, one tin, three dinner knives and a quarter box of tea in Barrow by Lancaster Sessions and sentenced to five years' penal servitude.

Ann had been lodging in Barrow with Mrs Jane Wood, a widow and keeper of a small shop, but after less than a week, she was turned out of the house for bad conduct. Later she was caught concealing items under her shawl, though claimed she had been given them. The Chairman read out a long list of her previous convictions against Ann and described her as an 'incorrigible rogue' (*Lancaster Gazette*, 20 October 1883).

After numerous short prison sentences, Ann now faced a five-year sentence and was removed from Lancaster Prison to Millbank in November 1883. In

1884 Ann received a letter from her husband, Joseph, but it was not given to her on account of a bad report from the police. Her prison records show numerous letters by prison officials who were trying to find her husband's whereabouts; a letter from a registrar stating that 'there was no marriage in the name of Gorst in or about November 1880', as well as letters from Liverpool police stating that the residents of Atholl Street denied knowing Ann. The prison administrators corresponded extensively with local police in order to ascertain the whereabouts of families of prisoners and most importantly to ensure that the people writing and receiving letters from the convicts were respectable or at the very least 'had nothing against them'. In July 1884 she was moved to Woking Prison and in December of the same year she eventually received a letter from her husband.

In February 1886, Ann was moved to Fulham Refuge and then she was released on conditional licence to East End House in May 1886; and permitted to leave the refuge sometime later. Her intention was to return to Barrow. In 1896 she received three months for stealing a shirt at Garston in Lancashire; her record stating that she also had over forty summary convictions for various offences. We lose track of Ann after her release but it is possible that she was convicted again under the name Ann Murphy but she did not breach her licence.

39. William Goss (born 1831, Ipswich, Suffolk) Licence no. 20655/ 22545

THE LANDING of the CONVICTS at BOTANY BAY

Eighteenth-century transported convicts
(*Authors' Collections*)

From the mid-seventeenth century onward, convicts were transported to some American colonies to complete their sentence. The 1718 Transportation Act increased the numbers sent across the Atlantic until the American Revolution curtailed this option. Australia then became the site of penal colonies (New South Wales initially, then to Van Diemen's Land – now Tasmania, then to Swan River – now Perth. Approximately 168,000 convicts were sent to Australia to serve some time in a penal work gang building roads and bridges and so on, before being released first on assignment to private employers, then on a ticket-of-leave, until finally earning their freedom.

William was an agricultural worker lodging in Hadleigh, near Ipswich in Suffolk in 1851. He was unmarried but had a two-year-old son that lived with the mother. On 3 January 1853 he was convicted of sheep-stealing and sentenced to seven years' transportation at Suffolk Sessions. He never made the journey to an Australian penal colony, but spent his sentence on British soil before being released to make a new life for himself.

William married the mother of his son, Elizabeth, but his efforts at reform seemed to have foundered because in 1861 he was convicted of larceny from the person of John Betts. In that case he pleaded not guilty on the grounds that he had had no intention of stealing from his friend John. He asserted that his friend had been drinking in a public house with him, had got a little tipsy, and was in danger of losing his coins, or of spending all his money on alcohol. He had merely saved his friend from this fate. However, in cross-examination, it appeared that his firm friend had only met him for the first time that day, and the Judge considered that William had been convicted on the clearest of evidence. He was sentenced to fifteen months, served in Ipswich Gaol.

The year 1866 was an eventful one for William. His daughter Emily was born, and, a few months later, he was convicted of larceny and the receiving of seven fleeces; and sentenced to five years at Guildford Sessions.

Again William believed there had been a miscarriage of justice, and wrote for legal advice to a barristers' office. Their reply stating that 'Mr Walpole sees no sufficient ground for interference in matter of Goss' reveals their dismissive view of convicts like William as much as their attitude towards the law: 'I trust the sentence was only a violation of law and not a defeat of justice'.

He continued to complain about his lot whilst in prison, and he committed a number of breaches of prison regulations (for which he was punished by losing remission, and serving time in solitary confinement on a penal diet). His breaches included: demanding a candle at the same time as having one concealed in his shoe; trafficking with bread; having his knife sharpened and shaving himself; having a quantity of salt and cheese in his cell; talking and having bread, cheese, meat and potatoes in his possession; and burying a prisoner's jacket in the ground. Despite losing remission he was released on licence with eleven months to serve in 1870.

On release William picked up work as a gardener in London. His wife and children remained in Suffolk. He was not living with his wife when the census was taken in 1881, and by 1891 she simply recorded herself as a widow, which in effect if not in law, she was.

40. **Moses Gould** (born 1820, Studland, Dorset) Licence no. 212

Ticket of Leave men, 1862 (*Henry Mayhew*, London Labour and the London Poor, *vol. III, 1861*)

There was a considerable stigma attached to such individuals who were in receipt of a licence or 'ticket-of-leave, and the suing of Moses Gould in October 1858 by an unpaid creditor, John Brett of Wareham, illustrates that there were also legal implications. Brett accused Gould of defaulting on payment of £3 2s. of goods sold to Gould's wife whilst Gould was serving his sentence of seven years' transportation. Gould's defence stated that in the eyes of the law he was civilly dead and therefore not responsible for the debt, but the judge (after admitting that this was the first case of its kind) agreed with the plaintiff in the full amount claimed.

Moses Gould was born at Studland in Dorset on 23 July 1820, the eldest of eight children, growing up to be an imposing figure of six feet two inches, with a scar over his right eye. In the 1841 census he is listed as a farm labourer, still living with his parents and siblings on their farm. Three years later he married Mary Ann Tocock at Marylebone, London and the couple eventually had six children (two being christened in Westminster).

At the age of 31 however, Moses Gould appears to have made a serious misjudgement. He was by this time a marine store dealer/boot and shoe dealer and cutter, employing two men at South Street, Wareham. On 15 October 1851 he was charged at Dorchester Criminal Court with having received a quantity of beef from Charles Parker and James Warren, knowing it to have been stolen. The manner of the accusation was unusual; Parker and Warren had just been found guilty of the theft of the beef when the prosecution solicitor stepped forward and accused Gould of receiving. Gould was subsequently remanded and appeared before the court again on Friday 17 October charged with both stealing and receiving the beef. The first count was dismissed, but he was found guilty of receiving and sentenced to transportation for ten years. He was first committed to Dorchester Gaol before being transferred to Millbank Prison on 26 March 1852. He was then variously transferred to Pentonville, Portsmouth and Dartmoor prisons.

In April 1853 he petitioned the Secretary of State for his release, stating that he was innocent of the offence and his petition was signed by over 80 individuals. Four or five 'respectable witnesses' were, according to the petition, prepared to swear that 'he was in his own house, employed chiefly in leather cutting from 2pm until 8pm' on the day that the offence was committed. Such a petition was not a rare occurrence, but rather more unusual is that a vehement and detailed rebuttal of the 'facts' stated in the petition appeared in a letter published in the *Dorset County Chronicle* of 30 June 1853, and written by Reverend Harry Far Yeatman, Chairman of the Dorset Quarter Sessions.

In his letter, Yeatman refutes all of Gould's claims; he proves that Gould was present around the time of the theft; that witnesses saw him talking to the two thieves; that his 'good character' was only stated at the time of the trial by his father – and that in fact the court had heard from the Governor of Dorset Gaol who had previously known Gould whilst they both worked at Millbank Penitentiary, and that Gould had left the prison as 'a warrant was out to apprehend him for misconduct'.

The result of the Reverend Yeatman's intervention was that Gould's petition was not allowed, but his sentence was commuted to seven years' transportation. He was eventually released early on licence on 12 December 1853. His first wife died and he remarried, eventually earning a living as a licensed barge waterman in Melcombe; and died in the summer of 1893 at Weymouth at the age of 73.

41. Mary Grealey (born 1844, Liverpool) Licence no. 45899/7579

Glasgow Prison (*Authors' Collections*)

Historically there had been eight prisons in Glasgow, but by 1840, they had all closed except the bridewell at Duke Street, also known as the North Prison, and the Burgh Prison at Glasgow Green, also known as the South Prison (this closed in 1862). Increased pressure on prison accommodation led to recommendations for a new prison to hold up to 1000 prisoners. The proposal led to the construction of a new prison, HMP Barlinnie, which opened in 1882 and was built between 1880 and 1886, consisting of four-storey cell blocks. Duke Street Prison remained open until the mid-1950s but from the 1880s only held female prisoners.

Mary Grealey spent the early part of her criminal career in Scotland. When she was about seventeen years old she spent five months in prison in Glasgow for theft and in the following years twelve months and then fifteen months in prison in Edinburgh for theft. In 1867, Glasgow Assizes sentenced her to seven years' penal servitude for larceny under the name Jane Clark. After being committed to Ayr Prison she then spent most of this sentence in Perth Prison where Scottish convicts underwent penal servitude.

Mary was released on licence in June 1872. She had multiple aliases, Mary Davitt, Mary Green, Ann MacDonald, and was convicted under all of these names in different places across Britain. In the following years she was convicted in Newcastle-upon-Tyne, Durham, Manchester and Salford, for larcenies, stealing boots, vagrancy, under the Prevention of Crimes Act; and for stealing a watch and guard; for each of these offences she spent between four and eight months in local prisons in these areas.

In January 1883 at Liverpool Sessions she was sentenced to seven years' penal servitude for stealing a purse containing fifteen shillings and sixpence from the person of Lawrence Almond. She was received at Millbank Prison. A more detailed record for this period shows that she wrote to her son and daughter-in-law in Newcastle as well as friends or family in Liverpool. She had two, possibly three children. The letters she sent to friends or family in Richmond Row in Liverpool, then a notoriously bad street, were suppressed on account of a bad police report. The Chief Constable stated that 35 Richmond Row was 'an eating house kept by Mrs Bethell, a resort for bad characters and she is not considered a respectable person'.

Newspaper reports on Mary also suggest that she had been in prison in Ireland as well as Scotland and England. In July 1883, she was received at Fulham Prison and worked in the laundry, an occupation she also undertook outside of prison. During her incarceration she wrote letters regularly, certainly to her children or those who were caring for them and to friends. She spent a short time in the prison infirmary with debility. She was well behaved in prison, only being admonished on two occasions; once for being unnecessarily troublesome when being moved wards and once for knocking and shouting at 3.00am.

Mary was removed from Fulham on a conditional licence and sent to the Russell House Refuge in January 1887, when she had three years of her sentence remaining. She was permitted to leave the refuge by the directors of the Convict Prison on 1 October 1887 and headed back to Liverpool. No subsequent trace of her life can be found.

42. **Margaret Grey** (born c.1840, Liverpool) Licence no. A44593/7572

Kate Hamilton's 'Night-house' (*Henry Mayhew*, London Labour and the London Poor, *vol. III, 1861*)

Prostitution has never been a criminal offence in England. However, both soliciting and running a brothel *is* illegal. In 1861 the social reformer Henry Mayhew defined brothels as 'houses where speculators board, dress, and feed women, living upon the farm of their persons'. Several brothels in London, such as the infamous 'night house' of Kate Hamilton, were extremely well-known amongst well-heeled 'gentlemen' looking for an adventurous night out, but not many brothels could aspire to such trappings of luxury. Most were simply rooms in lodging houses, where very poorly-paid working women would occasionally augment their wages. Many of the brothel-keepers, such as Margaret Grey, maintained a façade of middle-class respectability.

Margaret Grey née Spencer was born in Liverpool in c.1840. For the next forty years nothing is known of her life story. She married Joseph Grey (aka Gray) and in 1881 is living with him at 32 Hawke Street, Liverpool. There are also two step-children in the household, suggesting that Margaret had been previously married and subsequently widowed. Two years later, Margaret makes her one and only recorded appearance in court. On 18 December 1883, she, together with a woman named Ann Warren and a man named Thomas Laffan, were alleged to have become 'accessories after the fact' in the murder of a retired Navy pensioner named Richard Russell. Kate Williams, aged c.43, was charged with his murder. All of the accused were also charged with the theft of an overcoat and £14 in cash from Mr Russell.

The offence had taken place in Burgess Street, Liverpool, in a 'house of ill-fame' (a brothel). The three defendants had apparently taken out the injured Mr Russell to the street outside the brothel and then called the police, claiming that an unconscious drunk was lying in the street. They were remanded in gaol and appeared at Liverpool Assizes on 8 May, where it was proven that Mr Russell had met his death as a result from a blow to his head. Kate Williams was found guilty of his manslaughter and sentenced to five years' penal servitude, but the other three defendants were cleared of the charge of being accessories after the fact. However, they were all found guilty of the theft of the overcoat and money, with Grey receiving a sentence of five years' penal servitude.

She served most of her sentence at Millbank Prison, where she kept up a regular correspondence with various officials in order to find out about her two children. On 17 June 1884 her record states that she 'is anxious to ascertain how her two children are – they were taken to the workhouse in Liverpool and from there she believes were transferred to Kirkdale Industrial School'. Police reports contained in the prison licence folder state that they had information on her for the last five to six years but not before that; there was nothing against her prior to this conviction, her sobriety was described as fair, her livelihood – 'has kept brothels during last 5–6 years'. She was described as middle class, with the occupation of a brothel-keeper, and her habits of life were given as irregular. Her family was deemed respectable, but her associates were low prostitutes.

After being informed by the Governor of Kirkdale Industrial School that her children are well, she kept up a regular flow of letters to the Governor, asking about her children's health and progress. On 8 December 1886 she was given conditional licence to be removed to Russell House Refuge in Streatham, and on 6 September 1887 she was given permission to leave the refuge on licence. She probably died in Liverpool in 1893.

43. Ann Griffiths (born 1830, Manchester) Licence no. 45090/7541

George Pound's 'ragged' school
(*Authors' Collections*)

Ragged schools began in Portsmouth in 1818 when cobbler George Pound (left) began teaching poor children for free. York Ragged and Industrial School opened in 1849. The system was designed to inculcate habits of good work and industry in boys and girls that were in danger of starting a life of crime. Children convicted of crimes were taken to Reformatories; those that were beyond parental control, or were at risk of becoming offenders were sent to Industrial Schools. Boys trained in tailoring and gardening and often went into agricultural trades or local industries; whereas the girls often became domestic servants. In 1850 York Ragged and Industrial School moved to the old workhouse buildings. In 1876 the school became boys only, when girls like Ann's daughter Harriet were relocated. The school closed in 1921.

The newspapers had reported only one conviction for Ann Griffiths by her second conviction for theft in 1872. Yet her prison record at that time stated that she already had six previous convictions on her record. Her record also possibly revealed the reason why her antecedent criminal history is hard to track down, as she had several aliases (Ann Jane Griffiths, Maria Williams, Mary Jane Mulholland, Sarah Jane Holland, Caroline Whittaker, Sophie Williams). Ann was by now aged 43, and described as: 'five feet tall, blue eyes and red hair, married to husband Robert, one child, fresh complexion, a cut over each eyebrow and a cut on forehead, a natural mark below her right elbow, and two cuts on her left thumb'.

She followed this conviction with another in Manchester in November 1874 when she stole a purse and was imprisoned in Belle Vue Prison (Manchester) for six months. Another theft two years later saw her return to the same prison for another year. This was the first time she was recorded as being a common prostitute, and a number of convictions for being a disorderly prostitute followed over the next couple of years in her home town of Manchester. Possibly connected to her life as a prostitute, she was convicted of stealing £16. 10s. from a person at Manchester in June 1883. Her previous convictions increased the seriousness of the offence, and her punishment, and she was sentenced to five years' penal servitude, followed by three years' police supervision.

Her daughter Harriet was being looked after in various industrial schools in Yorkshire, and Ann took every opportunity to write to her. We don't know if Harriet was happy there, but her mother petitioned the authorities for her daughter to be kept in the industrial school whilst she herself was in prison. Ann wrote to the Lady Superintendent of the Girls' Industrial School at Marygate, York, and continued to correspond with her daughter until she was released on licence in November 1886, with nineteen months of her sentence unexpired.

Upon release she returned to Manchester, and the 1891 census states she was a 61-year-old charwoman, born in Salford, Manchester, living with daughter Harriet, a 21-year-old shirt-maker. In the ten years afterwards, Harriet may have got married and moved away for her mother was admitted to Manchester Workhouse. As is perhaps fitting for someone who had employed so many aliases, it is difficult to trace her death. She may have died in November 1900; or in 1916. Hopefully the time that she spent with her daughter outside of prison, and the correspondence with her whilst in prison had given Ann some comfort in her difficult life.

44. Mary Griffiths (born 1839, Manchester) Licence no. A45126/7542

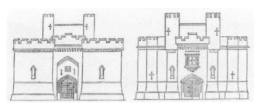

York Castle Prison Gatehouse (*Authors' Collections*)

With its characteristic medieval appearance, York Castle was developed into a formidable gaol. Re-built between 1825 and 1835 the site was an imposing fortress of punishment that dominated the City of York, before it became part of the national convict system in the 1850s. The prison was constructed in a radial plan, with the governor's residence at the hub of four wings that radiated outwards. Although it was a large and important convict establishment holding hundreds of prisoners, the prison was decommissioned in 1900, when it was converted into a military detention centre. It continued in that guise until it was closed in 1934. The prison now forms part of York Castle Museum.

Mary was brought before the Northampton courts in 1865 on three charges: 'larceny from the person, stealing purse and money, 2nd indictment for the like, third for the like'. Convicted of all three, she was sentenced to five years' penal servitude. On reception into Millbank, she was described as having 'a sallow complexion, dark brown hair, hazel eyes, five feet and half-an-inch, proportionate build, long face'.

On her release from prison she had scars on her forehead, right cheek, right arm, left eyebrow, ears pierced, lost several teeth. Part of the reason for that might be the considerable amount of violent confrontations that Mary experienced throughout her prison life. In 1866 she was punished for quarrelling and threatening to strike a fellow prisoner; and also for striking a prisoner on the head with a broom (she was kept in close confinement for two days and lost remission). The following year she received the same punishment for 'fighting a fellow prisoner and causing a great noise and confusion'; and for 'fighting and causing a great disturbance in the workroom'. Despite the loss of remission, she was released on conditional licence in March 1868.

Her time outside of prison did not last long. In October 1869 her licence was revoked and she was returned to Millbank Prison. When she was found quarrelling and fighting in the airing yard her punishment increased to one day in close confinement, but also one month in penal class and, in order to prevent further quarrel, she was ordered to exercise alone. However, there were other places to fight. In 1870 she lost her employment in the prison laundry for arguing with another laundry worker. She then lost her right to go to the Chapel for 'incessant talking in the chapel during service, causing disturbance'. The Chaplain fully concurred with the punishment. Her last punishment for fighting came in 1871, a couple of months before her sentence expired in November 1871.

Mary then had nearly a decade without troubling the courts. The stability she had found in her life was possibly then lost as she found herself prosecuted for vagrancy and pick-pocketing in 1880 (three offences committed at different times saw her imprisoned in local gaols for a total of just under six months). In 1883 she was sentenced to another five years at York Assizes. Her husband George was her accomplice, and he served eighteen months in York Castle Prison (where Mary was also kept for some of that time). On this sentence she was more passive in prison, and was only punished once (for being insolent about her work and having a piece of sharpened iron in her possession).

Mary was released on licence in 1886, her stated destination was Leeds, and she never re-offended again.

45. Francis J. Hammond (born 1839, Guernsey) Licence no. 85582/ 45473

Abortion was first made a criminal offence in 1803, but this Act only referred to abortions caused by the use of abortifacients (drugs), rather than those brought about by the use of instruments. This loophole was closed in 1828 and all forms of abortion were liable to the death penalty until 1837. In 1861 the Offences against the Person Act made the procuration of an abortion on a woman an offence liable to penal servitude for life, with the offence of supplying drugs in order to induce an abortion carrying a 5-year sentence. Abortion was finally legalised in Britain in 1967.

Headquarters of the Royal College of Surgeons (*Public Domain*)

Francis James Hammond's early life appears to have been relatively prosperous – by 1851 the family had moved to Sherborne in Dorset, and his father is listed as a retired East India Officer. At the age of 21 Francis graduated from university and was admitted as a Member of the Royal College of Surgeons in July 1860. In the 1861 census he is recorded as working as the Assistant Medical Officer at the Hampshire County Lunatic Asylum, Fareham, and he was also a member of the Royal College of Psychiatrists (later known as the Medico-Psychological Association).

It is not known when Hammond left his employment at the Lunatic Asylum, but he appears to have set up an unsuccessful practice in London which was declared bankrupt in 1867. Around this time he married Maria and by 1871 they were living in Howden, Yorkshire, together with two children. He is listed in the 1871 census as a General Practitioner. However, this practice also proved unsuccessful and he left Howden in debt. He moved to London, where he set up a joint practice with James Frederick Nottingham. This partnership was dissolved in May 1875 but Hammond seems to have continued practising on his own.

On 15 September 1879 he appeared at the Old Bailey, charged with procuring an abortion by means of an instrument on a young woman named Ellen Saunders. The case generated many column inches of newspaper reports as it emerged that Miss Saunders was Hammond's mistress – the couple had been living together as Mr and Mrs Saunders following what Hammond called 'some unpleasantness between him and his wife'. At the time of his arrest he also stated that 'this will be a fearful exposure for my wife and children and will ruin me in my business'.

Saunders had originally approached Hammond for help after she had found that she was pregnant, and the couple began a relationship. She had a baby and then became pregnant by Hammond, who subsequently carried out an abortion on her. A half-sister of Saunders, Amy Philips was thought to have informed the police that such an operation had been carried out, and Hammond was subsequently brought before Bow Street magistrates. A report conducted by Scotland Yard into Hammond's background later reported that 'It was disclosed in his trial that he was a very immoral man and that it is likely that he has procured the abortion of more than one woman'. Hammond was sentenced to ten years' penal servitude.

He remained in touch with his wife until she died in April 1885. Hammond was released after serving seven years and eight months of his sentence. He had petitioned on numerous occasions to be allowed books in prison in order to maintain his professional knowledge and is last recorded as a physician's assistant in Westminster in 1891. His date of death is unknown.

46. Joseph Hazell (born c.1833, Birmingham) Licence no. 355/5/22446

Based on the Royal Prerogative of Mercy, Free Pardons could (and still can) be granted by the reigning monarch. The Royal Prerogative of Mercy is defined as 'a common law extrajudicial power exercised by the Crown'. Three options can be exercised under this power:
• A free, unconditional pardon
• A conditional pardon, in which a lesser sentence is served instead of the original penalty
• Remission or partial remission of a sentence being served. At the time of the granting of Hazell's Free Pardon, it was in practice the Home Secretary who decided on the granting or otherwise of such a pardon – the monarch usually just signed the decree.

Queen Victoria (1819-1901)
(*Authors' Collections*)

Joseph Hazell was destined to have a troubled and violent life. His first recorded appearance in the criminal justice system was in March 1851, when he was found guilty of wounding with intent at Warwickshire Assizes, and sentenced to ten years' transportation. This probably was not his first brush with the law however, as he is recorded as having seven stars tattooed between his left thumb and forefinger – this type of marking usually signified either membership of a criminal gang or that he had previously been incarcerated. He appears to have had something of a lucky break in October 1853, when he was released from Portsmouth Prison after serving just over two-and-a-half years in gaol. In that year, the Penal Servitude Act was passed. This Act substituted penal servitude for some sentences of transportation, as Australia was becoming increasingly hostile to the continued influx of Britain's offenders to its shores. Many convicts awaiting transportation were instead granted conditional pardons, and Hazell walked out of Portsmouth Prison a free man on 20 October 1853.

A year later Joseph had returned to Birmingham and married Sarah Robinson. He appears to have kept his nose clean for a number of years, but in January 1859 he is found guilty of the first of what transpired to be a number of charges of assault. He was sentenced to three months' imprisonment, but offended again in the October of the following year, and was sentenced to two months.

Six months later he was found guilty of warehouse-breaking in Birmingham and sentenced to two years' imprisonment. Several assault offences followed his release (mostly on his wife, Sarah) and in July 1866 he stabbed a police constable who was in the process of arresting him on a charge of assaulting his wife yet again. Hazell was sentenced to five years' penal servitude. He was released on licence on 16 July 1870 with one year of his sentence unserved.

His long-suffering wife was once more the recipient of his temper in 1874, when he stabbed her in the back of the head. Mrs Hazell stated that 'she had been subjected to his ill-usage for the past twenty years, but did not wish him sent to prison'. The magistrate did not agree and sent him to prison for two months.

Age appears to have burnt his temper out, and he did not trouble the courts again, dying in 1896.

47. Mary Ann Hebden (born 1840, Bridlington Quay, Yorkshire) Licence no. A36958/7553

Victorian Scarborough (*Authors' Collections*)

Scarborough Police were asked to check up on Mary Ann's correct surname - Hebden or Dring. Prison authorities often sent out requests for further information as to the convict's character, and the respectability or otherwise of their friends and acquaintances. Scarborough Police replied that her correct surname was Hebden: 'Her husband, Samuel Hebden is a joiner and has lived with her in this town until 1876. After she came out of Gaol in 1878 she went to reside in Bridlington after that we lost trace of her until she turned up at Great Grimsby QS. We were not sorry when she left Scarborough because she was a dangerous character to be at large.'

Mary Ann Hebden (née Whitfield) was the daughter of an innkeeper of Bridlington Quay, where Mary lived until 1858, when she married joiner Samuel Hebden at Scarborough in the first quarter of 1858. Two children quickly followed and in the 1861 census Mary and Samuel are recorded as living in Scarborough. Mary and Samuel appear to have lived a stable family life for the first decade or so of their marriage, producing four more surviving children; and in the 1861 census Samuel was recorded as still following the trade of joiner and the family were still living in Scarborough.

However, the following year Mary made the first of many appearances in court, charged with the theft of a jacket in Scarborough, for which she received six months' imprisonment. The following year she appeared in the same court once more, this time charged with obtaining a watch by false pretences. She is described at this time as a charwoman, and received a sentence of nine months' imprisonment. In December of the following year she appeared at court again, charged with stealing an oil cloth and a lady's jacket. Newspaper reports state that she was charged with a total of nine robberies, and was found 'respectably dressed' but with a 'large number of pawn tickets in her pocket', suggesting that she was pawning the stolen goods. She offended with another woman named Mary Peacock. She received eighteen months' imprisonment and three years' police supervision.

She was released from prison on 28 June, but in August Mary once again found herself in court, receiving a sentence of eighteen months' imprisonment and five years' police supervision for stealing various items from a drapers. Mary and Samuel appear to have parted company shortly after this offence, as Samuel is recorded as lodging in Scarborough without Mary in the 1881 census. In April 1884 Mary appears yet again in court, this time charged with larceny as a servant of clothing belonging to Reverend William Butler in Belleau, Lincolnshire. She had been employed as the Reverend's cook. She appeared with a man called Henry Dring, who was described as her 'husband', and who was gardener to Reverend Butler. It is clear that they were by this time living together as man and wife (despite Mary's husband Samuel still being alive). Henry Dring received a sentence of three months as Mary was thought to be the driving force behind the offence.

Mary was sentenced to five years' penal servitude, spending her time in both Millbank and Woking prisons. On 16 November 1886 she was issued with a conditional licence to be removed to Russell House Refuge, Streatham, from where she was released on licence on 13 August 1887. She then disappears from record, but a Mary Ann Hebden is recorded as dying in Hull in 1916 at the age of 74; it is possible that this is the same woman. Her husband Samuel remarried, appearing in the 1911 census as a retired joiner, aged 76; he is recorded as living with Isabella, aged 68, his wife of seven years.

48. Martha Hedger (born 1831, Bath) Licence no. 26621/7543

Victorian policemen (*Authors' Collections*)

The Lambeth Police Court (later Lambeth Magistrates' Court) was opened in1869 to operate as a court of summary justice, delivering cheap and available justice for a growing part of London. Minor offenders received up to one year's custody from local magistrates (later a paid stipendiary magistrate was appointed to the court), and the more serious offenders were committed up to the Old Bailey for trial or sentence. Lambeth Police Court was conveniently situated next to Kennington Lane Police Station, and together they formed the heart of the criminal justice system in Lambeth. The court was closed in the 1990s with its work transferred to Camberwell Green Magistrates' Court; and the buildings are now used as a centre for Buddhism.

Martha was a married woman with three children, and a working husband, when she was first convicted at Lambeth Police Court. She was twice gaoled for stealing clothes in 1863. A further twelve months' custody followed the next year. In 1867 she received her first bout of penal servitude when she was convicted of stealing trousers in Lambeth. She started her five-year sentence when she was pregnant, and miscarried soon after entering prison. In 1869 she petitioned the Governor to change her religion, on the grounds that it had been her father's last wish on his death bed that she remain a Catholic. However, having previously told the prison authorities that she was a Protestant, the Governor refused her petition. The following year she was released on licence via Battery House Refuge.

She was re-convicted the following year for stealing bread and for gaining goods by false pretences, and she entered another five-year sentence. This time, Martha told the prison authorities that she was a Roman Catholic. However, she then petitioned the Governor to be allowed to change her religion. She said that she registered herself Catholic to please herself and she now wishes to be registered a Protestant to please herself. She, however, at the same time also stated that she never cared for any religion and never did. With that declaration, her petition was refused. The next time she made a similar request it was because her parents 'are Protestant and she wishes to follow the same faith'. The authorities asked her husband which religion Martha had been brought up in; he replied, 'Sir, my wife was brought up as a Cartherlic' [sic].' She then petitioned the authorities to reduce her sentence because she had committed it through destitution. Indeed, her frequent petitions throw considerable light upon the reasons why she fell into prison so frequently.

In 1873 she petitioned for early release on the grounds that her present sentence was inflicted for falsely claiming poor relief on the grounds that her husband had left her and the children (when he was merely unemployed). The request was refused. The following year a similar request fell on deaf ears: 'Was not aware of the gravity of her offence. Her children are in want and her husband only in partial work. Husband willing to receive her. No Grounds.' When she was released on licence she was soon re-convicted for theft, and also made a number of petitions during that ten-year sentence. These petitions alleged that alcohol addiction had caused her to steal, and that she was prepared to live a life of sobriety. All of her requests were refused until she was released after serving seven years in convict prisons (in 1886). Her husband was living in Newington Workhouse, and she died in 1891, in St Olave's Workhouse.

49. Sarah Jane Howlett (born 1844, Bradford) Licence no. A45211/7544

> *The permission to write and receive Letters is given to Convicts for the purpose of enabling them to keep up a connection with their respectable friends, and not that they may hear news of the day.*
>
> *All letter are read by the Prison authorities … Any which are of an objectionable tendency, either to or from Convicts, or containing slang, or improper expressions, will be suppressed.*

(*Prison Rule 341c [1881]*)

Sarah grew up with her family in Bradford, where her father was a shoemaker. By her seventeenth birthday, however, her mother had died, and shortly afterwards her grandparents moved in to house together with Sarah, her father, her siblings, and also her married sister and her husband. The family may have clung together for support, or to save money in difficult times. This might explain Sarah's first offence – stealing a shirt in Sheffield in 1867 (for which she received a two–month prison sentence). It may also have been because Sarah's father had re-married, and, in 1871, was living with his wife in a large lodging house with multiple families on Bolton Road, Bradford. Neither Sarah nor any of her siblings were living with their father.

Prisoners were allowed to send letters periodically. However, if the recipient was 'known' to the police, lived in a place frequented by thieves or prostitutes, or was a serving prisoner (or after being investigated by the local police force just found to be an unsuitable correspondent) the letters were kept on file and never delivered. Letters that were 'suppressed' reveal details of a prisoner's home life that would otherwise be lost, and so do letters that passed between official authorities, for example the ones that passed between the various convict prison Governors and the religious bodies in determining Sarah's previous religious affiliation.

In 1874 Sarah and an accomplice dragged a drunken unemployed groom into a backyard and robbed him of his money. Described in the newspaper as a 'garrotting' (similar to a mugging, involving strangulation), Sarah's previous convictions also told against her, and she was sentenced to twelve months prison and three years police supervision at Leeds Assizes.

Under police supervision she was required to report fortnightly to the local police station, and to keep the police informed of where she was living. Sarah breached her conditions in 1876 and received a two-week prison sentence (under the 1871 Prevention of Crimes Act); and in 1880 her second breach meant a further twelve-month sentence. In June 1882 she served another month for theft from the person, but 1884 saw her receive her first long sentence. She was committed at Bradford Sessions for stealing thirteen shillings from the person and ordered to serve five years' penal servitude and five years' police supervision.

Sarah entered convict prison as a Catholic, but then applied to become Protestant. The priest replied: 'I believe this woman to be a Protestant and further I believe that she did not enrol herself as a Catholic on entering the prison from any sincere religious motive.' The Protestant Chaplain agreed: 'This prisoner's statements go to prove that she is a protestant by birth and training and that all of her relatives are protestant or non-conformists. She was induced to declare herself R.C. by a prisoners trick at the same Sessions with herself. She is decidedly unhappy at being obliged to attend R.C. services which she does not understand.' The Prison Governor then made enquiries amongst her neighbours and family in Bradford without response. Nevertheless, her application was approved.

The same year as her father died (1886), Sarah was released on conditional licence with nearly two and a half years left of her sentence. In 1891 she was a lodger and charwoman, and she died in Bradford in 1920, aged 69.

50. Mary Howley (born c.1821, County Mayo) Licence 7439

The parish was the most basic form of local government in England. Each parish was legally responsible for the poor relief of its parishioners. Oversight of such relief developed on a piecemeal basis, but many parishes appointed a Parish Overseer of the Poor (aka Receiving Officer), and who as his title suggests, doled out small amounts of financial aid to the deserving poor who could claim the parish as their birthplace. Such individuals were often deeply unpopular. From 1846, following the passing of the Five Years Residential Act, anyone could claim relief if they could prove five years' continuous residence in the same parish. Mary must have done this, as she was born in Ireland.

Extract from parish overseer's book
(*Authors' Collections*)

By her mid-twenties Mary had emigrated to Liverpool, where she first appears before the courts in July 1846 charged with an unrecorded offence, for which she received a sentence of eleven months' imprisonment. In 1849 she was found guilty of falsely claiming parish relief as a widow from the Liverpool Parish Relieving Officer (her husband John Gardner was still alive), and sentenced to two months' imprisonment.

Over the next four years she committed several more petty offences, receiving short prison sentences, but in May 1853 she was found guilty of stealing a frock at Liverpool, and as a result of her long list of previous offences, she was sentenced to ten years' transportation. However, in the same year the Penal Servitude Act was passed, effectively severely limiting the number of people who were actually sent abroad to serve their sentence, and it appears that Mary was one of many women who stayed in an English prison. She was released on licence sometime within the next four-and-a-half years, as she appears once more in court records in October 1857, charged with stealing eighteen yards of carpet in Liverpool. She received a sentence of seven years' penal servitude, but this did not reform her, and in June 1867 she appeared at the Liverpool Sessions again, charged with a pan, a shirt and three towels, for which she received ten years' penal servitude. She is by this time described as 'an old offender' and her occupation is given as 'hawker' (a mobile trader) – an often precarious and hand-to-mouth existence.

After serving seven years of this sentence she was released early on licence on 24 June 1873 to the East End Refuge in Finchley, London. This was a 'halfway house' for 'distressed Roman Catholic women', first created in 1864 by the Sisters of the Good Shepherd. Female prisoners close to discharge would be sent there in order to get them acclimatised to release. However, this rehabilitation failed in Mary's case and she returned to Liverpool, where she again offended in July 1875, being sentenced to twelve months' imprisonment for theft.

She must have committed another offence in the following year, as she is recorded as being committed to Millbank in July 1876. By this time she was beginning to show her advancing years; she spent much of her time in Woking Female Invalid Prison after being transferred there in April 1877 with rheumatism. On 15 June 1880 she was released and once more returned to Liverpool. Mary committed one final offence in August 1881, being found guilty of stealing two coats. She received a sentence of seven years' penal servitude. She was released on licence on 29 May 1886. Her last known residence was in fact recorded in the 1891 census, where she is listed as a pauper inmate of Whiston Workhouse in Lancashire.

51. Elizabeth Hyde (born 1838, St Germans, Cornwall) Licence no. 83720/ 7580

Exeter Gaol (*Authors' Collections*)

Exeter Gaol and House of Correction was built between 1790 and 1794 during the period of prison reform as the county gaol for Devon. It was designed by prominent prison architect, William Blackburn and contained 136 cells. A new gatehouse was built in 1807-9 and three wings on a radial design. A new prison was built on North Road in 1853 by John Hayward another prominent prison architect, drawing on the radial prison on a cruciform design that was common for the mid-nineteenth century. HMP Exeter still operates on the same site today as a local prison for male adults and young offenders, holding over 500 prisoners.

Elizabeth Hyde served two sentences of penal servitude during her life but she did not commit her first offence until she was in her late thirties. Elizabeth was born and grew up in Cornwall; born Elizabeth Wills, she married William Hyde when she was about 19 years old. All seemed to be well with the family; in the early 1870s, they had a farm with 100 acres employing one man and two boys as well as a domestic servant and two farm servants. By this time Elizabeth's mother was also living with them. It is not clear what happened to the family circumstances but after Elizabeth's mother's death, things seemed to turn for the worse. By October 1876, at the age of 38, Elizabeth had been convicted of obtaining money under false pretences and was sentenced to five years' penal servitude. She was sent to Millbank and then on to Woking where she worked as a 'tailoress'. By this time, William and the family were living in Plymouth. After serving just over half of her sentence, Elizabeth was released on conditional licence and sent to Battery House Refuge, arrived there at the end of May 1879. She was permitted to leave the Refuge at the end of February the following year.

Elizabeth returned to Plymouth to reside with William and her children but by May 1881 she was back in court. At Exeter Assizes she pleaded guilty, due to destitution, of forging bills or securities for the sums of £12, £15, and ten shillings and two pence, and she was subsequently sentenced to seven years' penal servitude. Again Elizabeth went to Millbank from Exeter Prison and then in November to Fulham Prison where she undertook needlework. In addition to the seven-year sentence, she would also have to serve the remnant of her previous sentence.

In Plymouth family circumstances were very difficult for William and the children. Elizabeth was granted permission to write letters to inquire about getting two of her daughters into school at the Princess Mary Village Home. The district visitor wrote stating that the children were in a deplorable condition and it was impossible to do anything for them.

The Prison Mission were unable to help the family as William was employed. He worked as a tram-car driver but they now had at least nine children, though the older children were working, five were under twelve years old and they found it difficult to cope. Elizabeth regularly wrote and received letters from William and she was visited by a cousin every three to four months. Elizabeth also petitioned a number of times to be released early, pleading that her family needed her at home.

Elizabeth was not successful until 4 January 1887 when she was released on licence 'to be at large' and returned to her family. She did not commit any further offences.

52. Julia Hyland (born 1854, Wigan) Licence no. A46066/7581

The straitjacket, along with cross-chains and a canvas dress, was intended to be a punishment as well as a restraint on prisoners deemed dangerous to the prison authorities. Prisoners such as Julia, who had attacked fellow prisoners as well as prison staff (she stabbed the Medical Officer in the back of his neck on one occasion) experienced the straitjacket on many occasions. The straps tied the prisoner in with their arms by their sides, unable to move. No doubt effective, the restraints would have also been extremely uncomfortable (and painful if they struggled) as well as humiliating. Prisons still used the straitjacket as a means of control into the 1960s.

Harry Houdini, the escapologist, in a straitjacket (*Authors' Collections*)

Julia was first imprisoned in 1868, for being drunk and riotous in her home city of Manchester. At that time she was a single woman with one child, living with her parents in Ancoats. In March 1871 she was imprisoned for two months as 'Julia Hiland' for stealing linen; and by December she was back inside for stealing sheets, this time under the name of Julia Hardman, having married John Hardman in the autumn.

Nine months passed before she was re-convicted in 1872 for stealing clothes, and given twelve months' custody followed by seven years police supervision (as a habitual offender having committed two indictable offences by this time). Police supervision did not deter her from offending and she received several sentences for drunkenness until 1875 when she received her first sentence of penal servitude. She was convicted of theft of oilcloth and sentenced to seven years' prison and a further seven years' police supervision on her release.

She was not a model prisoner. Whilst in prison Julia breached regulations by fighting with other prisoners, shouting, swearing, breaking prison property, threatening staff, attacking warders and matrons, threatening to commit suicide, malingering, threatening the medical officer, and so on. Indeed she was punished for forty-seven separate breaches of rules on her first long prison sentence, having been restrained in a straitjacket on frequent occasions.

The Roman Catholic priest at Millbank stated: 'I am afraid that the prisoner is perfectly responsible for her actions and is simply wicked'; a view confirmed by the Medical Officer: '… soon after her arrival in Millbank she "broke out" and it was only after effectual restraint in jacket and ankle straps that she was subdued. For many weeks past she has been more manageable, although it has been necessary to grant her some indulgence in her diet. She is passionate, wilful, and impatient, and she complained much of pain in the top of her head…her general health is good but she is subject to occasional outbursts of violent temper during which she is dangerous. Her disposition is treacherous, so that in dealing with her it is well to be guarded.'

Released in July 1882, she was quickly re-convicted in February 1882 for the theft of a frying pan in Manchester and sentenced to another seven years' penal servitude. Before she was released in 1886, with three years of her sentence yet to go, she had only breached prison regulations three times. The fight shown in her first bout of penal servitude seemed to have been extinguished by the time she started her second time in the convict system.

53. Eliza Ingamells (born c.1833, Leake, Lincolnshire) Licence no. A46814/ 7625

Female prison laundry (*H. Mayhew and J. Binny,* The Criminal Prisons of London and Scenes of London Life, *1862*)

In 1881 whilst Elizabeth was undergoing the first of several prison terms at Spalding Gaol, the Governor and Matron of the prison were a married couple, James and Emma Higgins. This husband and wife combination was a fairly usual set-up in Victorian prisons. Spalding Prison originated as a House of Correction in 1619, designed to house 'rogues and vagabonds' who were set to work within its walls. The House of Correction was demolished in 1834 and in 1836 Spalding Prison opened its doors. Female prisoners such as Elizabeth (who was a seamstress by trade) would have worked at sewing or in the prison laundry.

At the age of eight Elizabeth is recorded as living at Firth Ville, less than five miles away from the home of her future husband, Robert Ingamells (they shared the same surname and may have been cousins). Ten years later in 1851 she is recorded as a house servant to Robert's family at West Fen, Boston. Robert's father, Joseph, was a farmer of some 85 acres and was obviously wealthy enough to employ domestic help for his wife, Eleanor.

Three years later, Eliza and Robert were married and the first of their children, Ellen, was born. Her family may have fallen victim to one of the numerous agricultural depressions of the mid-Victorian period – in 1861 she is recorded as living on parochial allotments at Leake, with Robert (described as a farm labourer). On 30 December of that year she and Robert both appeared before Boston Quarter Sessions magistrates on a charge of stealing lard and two lots of clothing. Robert was given nine months for all three charges, whilst Eliza received concurrent sentences of six months and two of nine months. These offences may have been the result of increased poverty; farm labourers were notoriously poorly paid. Whatever the reason, Eliza kept out of trouble for the next twenty years, despite being widowed in 1873.

However, in 1881, Eliza made another appearance before magistrates, this time charged with stealing a bottle of brandy. Her co-accused was her eldest daughter Ellen (who was by this time married. Ellen received four months' imprisonment, whilst Eliza was sentenced to eighteen months. In the 1881 census she appears as a prisoner in Spalding Gaol, with the occupation of seamstress (another poorly paid occupation). Her daughter Ellen appears immediately above her in the list of inmates.

Two years later, Eliza appears before the Boston Quarter Sessions magistrates on two occasions, being sentenced to four months for stealing jam; and in December to five years' penal servitude for stealing clothes. Her accomplices in the latter crime were her eldest daughter Ellen and her third daughter, Fanny (who was married at the time). Eliza's daughters received sentences of six months and two months respectively. After initially spending time at Spalding Gaol, she was transferred to Millbank in January 1884, where she spent the next six months, before being transferred to Woking, as she had been suffering from both a prolapsed uterus and chronic diarrhoea, for which she was treated with tincture of opium and beef tea. Whilst at Woking, Eliza kept up a regular correspondence with her daughter Fanny. In 1887 her eldest daughter Ellen was again imprisoned, this time for a period of six months on a charge of larceny. On 30 April 1887 Eliza received a licence, remitting one year and seven months of her sentence, and was released to 2 Union Street, Boston. In 1901 she received three months for stealing tins of lobster, having also been twice fined for indecent language in 1896 and 1897, and in 1904 at the age of 70 she was discharged with a caution after stealing two drinking glasses in Boston.

54. Thorborg Ireland (born 1825, Norway) Licence no. 3607

Newcastle Gaol and House of Correction was located in Carliol Square between 1823-8. It was a detached radial design, common at the time, with six wings. The new gaol was designed by John Dobson and replaced an old borough gaol which existed at Newgate. Wings were added in the 1850s and 1860s and further expansion occurred in 1871. However, the prison only operated for about ninety years as it was closed in 1925. The Prison Commissioners had wanted to close the site for a number of years as they regarded it unsuitable, but they had been unable to do so due to the size of the prison population. It was one of seven prisons closed between 1925 and 1931. All of the prisoners were removed to HMP Durham.

Visiting a prisoner
(*Authors' Collections*)

James and Thorborg Ireland lived in Dundee in 1851. Thorborg had been born in Christianson, Norway, her maiden name was Henderson, and James was a ship's master from Dundee. By 1860 they had had four children and in the summer of that year another child, John was born. However, on 27 December 1860 tragedy struck when James was lost at sea. His ship, *Twin Brothers*, was lost off the coast of Newcastle and he was presumed drowned. In 1861, Thorborg was keeping a beershop on Castle Street, Monifieth, Angus, living with her five children, a female domestic servant and a gentleman. In 1864, further tragedy occurred when her 14-year-old daughter Helena died.

In October 1866, Thorborg was committed to Newcastle Prison having been charged with arson; more specifically, setting fire to a house in order to defraud the insurance company. She had no previous convictions or brushes with the law, but perhaps the circumstances she found herself in after the death of her husband give some context for her actions. It was claimed that she had set fire to the beer shop that she kept, in order to draw on two insurance policies, each for £100.

At the assizes in Newcastle-upon-Tyne, it was stated that she had tried to pay a former servant to set fire to the house and cut the gas pipe when it was done. A current servant stated that she had placed wood shavings around the house and that she had sent the servant to a neighbours with a box containing all of the insurance documents. The policeman who arrived at the scene supported these claims, stating that wood shavings and tarred sticks had been placed about the house and the fire had been started in five different places. Thorborg denied the charge, but the jury found her guilty and she was sentenced to five years' penal servitude.

After an initial period at Newcastle Prison, Thorborg arrived at Millbank in May 1867. She was a well-behaved prisoner; in the course of her incarceration she was only admonished once, for 'standing out of place in the airing yard'. She wrote and received letters when the rules permitted her, no doubt to and from her children. She was transferred to Brixton Prison in November 1867 and during her time she also received a regular visit. We are not sure who visited her, but it was often the case that those convicts who were not from the south of England, did not ever receive visitors, even when they were permitted them. Thorborg was transferred to Fulham Refuge in June 1869 and released on licence in July 1870 through the DPAS (Discharged Prisoners' Aid Society).

Thorburg did not commit any further crimes during her life. In 1871 she was living and working as a nurse in Newcastle-upon-Tyne infirmary. She died, aged 60 at Tynemouth in 1880.

55. Sarah Jemmison (born 1832, Danby, Yorkshire) Licence no. 3696

Female convicts (*Authors' Collections*)

The Assize courts that originated in the twelfth century were the highest criminal courts, which dealt with serious offences until they were abolished in 1971. York Assizes were part of the Northern Circuit. Judges perambulated around York, Durham, and Lancaster holding summer and winter Sessions in turn. The Assizes were grand and solemn affairs, but were often described as a circus since a retinue of lawyers, solicitors, journalists, and others always accompanied the Judges. In York, Sarah would have appeared before this grand circus in an elegant courthouse designed in the 1770s. The whole affair must have been terrifying for the young woman from a small Yorkshire village.

Sarah's mother died when Sarah was only 14, leaving her and her widowed father to fend for themselves. He was described as a pauper and agricultural labourer in the 1851 census. The family eked out a living in Yorkshire, and life was probably not easy. In 1857 things got much worse when Sarah was sentenced to death for the infanticide of her 3-year-old son. The sentence was later commuted to a life-term in prison.

Sarah was perhaps fortunate not to hang for her offence. The body of her son had been found in several pieces on the Yorkshire moors, with the body showing signs of considerable brutality. Had Sarah callously assaulted and tortured the boy before killing him and burying him on the moors? That was the case the prosecution made, and they demanded the death penalty for this heinous crime. The circumstantial evidence also looked bad for Sarah. After gaining a job in domestic service, Sarah had arranged for a nurse to look after her child whilst she was at work, the child residing with the nurse. However, she could not keep up the payments and she was forced to take the child to live with her in service. When her employer objected to this arrangement she offered to take the child to a nurse. She set out with the child on a donkey across the moors, and returned alone. When a dog discovered a child's leg, an attending constable dug around the moors until he found a child's skull, thigh, and some ribs.

Sarah's defence was that she had abandoned the child on the moors hoping that someone would find him, and take him in. She maintained that she had not killed him, the environment has, and wild animals must have disfigured the body *post mortem*. Considerable legal and medical debate followed as to how the child received his injuries, and there was enough sympathy both for Sarah's explanation and for circumstances that her sentence was commuted.

Whilst in jail, Sarah was a model prisoner. She committed no breaches of prison regulations – a rare situation, since even very compliant convicts could easily pick up one or two prison offences. A note on her penal record in 1869 states that her case was 'to be brought forward for consideration of the Sec of State when she has undergone 13 years and 4 months from date of conviction'. She was, in fact, given early release on licence the following year.

The 1871 census records her as working as a domestic servant to a widower in Yorkshire. She was employed as a nanny to his four small children, and she continued to be employed in domestic service until she died in Yorkshire in 1898 aged 65. She never married, and she never gave birth to another child.

56. Edith Jennings (born 1868, Bromsgrove, Worcestershire) Licence no. A41971/7559

Women under separate confinement were employed coir-picking as well as rough sewing and bag-making. At the public works stage they worked in the laundries and at needlework and sewing. They undertook all of the washing for the staff and for themselves. They also did all of the washing for the male convicts at Millbank and Pentonville. They did all of the needlework for the whole convict prison system. At Fulham and Woking prisons they undertook training in domestic service as well as baking, cooking and housework. Some female prisoners were also employed as farm servants or in gardening and others in mosaic tiling. They also did the washing for other convict prisons.

Edith Jennings, aged 18
(*The National Archives*)

Edith Jennings was 17 years old and had been working as a servant for two or three months at Tardebiggs, near Redditch in 1885, when she was charged with setting fire to a number of haystacks. She was committed to the assizes by Redditch magistrates but released on bail. The ricks of hay that were burnt were the property of her employer, Mr Herbert French, of Wright's Farm, and had been set alight on 23 and 24 August. It was estimated that sixty tonnes of hay had been destroyed, having a value of about £160, though the property was not insured. After initially blaming a man passing by, she admitted the offence to her employers and the police, but she could not say why she had done it. Edith's father, William was an active member of the local fire brigade and had narrowly escaped injury at the first fire as he had been on the rick when it fell. At Gloucester Assizes, at the end of October 1885, the judge thought this was a serious offence that was increasing in commission. The judge acknowledged that the prisoner had raised the alarm and her father had assisted in putting out the fire, but stated the crime had been committed in secret and she had tried to implicate someone else. In November, the court sentenced Edith to five years' penal servitude.

Edith was committed first to the local prison at Worcester and then in February sent to Woking Prison. She was categorised as 'Star Class' as she had no previous convictions and no criminal connections. In the same month, the Governor was asked by the Home Office to prepare a report on her conduct before fifteen months of her sentence had been served. The following October, Edith's case again appeared in the newspapers; a petition had been raised for her release based on claims that the sentence was too severe. The petitioners noted that Edith was the daughter of respectable parents and the petition had been signed by the whole of the Redditch magistrates bench, Lord Windsor, Mr French (the prosecutor and her former employer) and upwards of 1,000 of the principal 'manufacturers etc' of the town and district. It was claimed that the offences had been committed due to hysteria. In mid-November 1886, the High Sheriff of Worcestershire, Mr Victor Milward, received a letter from the Home Secretary announcing that due to the very special circumstances of Edith's case he had authorised her release from Fulham Prison on licence. She would be discharged as soon as practicable. Edith was released on licence to be at large on 19 November and returned to her family home in Redditch; she had served thirteen months of her five-year sentence in prison. In 1891 she was living with her aunt's family in West Ham, London and working as a parlour maid.

57. Mary Ann Johnson (born 1853, St Giles, London) Licence no. A45421/7562

Prison education (*H. Mayhew and J. Binny,*
The Criminal Prisons of London and Scenes of
London Life, *1862*)

Basic education in prison has existed for at least two hundred years. After the 'reform' period, prisoners were taught religious texts and tracts by the chaplain of the prison. Chaplains had to be appointed in all prisons from 1823 onwards, in addition in larger prisons, the chaplain was often supported by a schoolmaster who would carry out basic education classes such as reading and writing and the alphabet as well as religious readings and lectures. By the mid-nineteenth century, prisoners were taught to read and write to varying degrees and their level of literacy was assessed on entry to the convict system. Convicts also had to show some ability of reading and writing in order to be able to progress through the stage system.

Mary Ann Johnson or Heard (her maiden name) was convicted at the Central Criminal Court in 1884 for unlawfully uttering counterfeit coin and sentenced to five years' penal servitude. Witnesses for the prosecution stated that Mary had gone into The Globe public house in Euston Square and tried to pay for half a pint of beer with a 'bad' half-crown. The landlord's daughter who served Mary immediately saw the coin was 'bad' and told her father. The landlord challenged Mary who said she did not know what he meant and he bent the coin under the beer pull. The 'potman' had seen Mary in the bar with a dog and outside of the pub with three men; he had also seen one of the men give the coin to Mary.

John Chapple, policeman, took Mary into custody for attempting to pass the coin. She said she had been given it by three men and gave the names of two of them at the police station as Johnson and Jones. She refused to give her address to the inspector. In her statement to the magistrate and in her defence Mary stated that she had met the three men and asked one of them to lend her a shilling; he had given her half a crown (two shillings and sixpence) to get change. She was then found guilty and pleaded guilty to a previous offence of uttering counterfeit coin in March 1883. Although this was Mary's second coining offence, she had also been in trouble with the law a few years earlier when she served six weeks in prison for assault in 1875 and four months in prison for stealing a gold locket in 1876. This time her offences would result in a much longer period of incarceration.

On entering Millbank Prison for the period of separation, Mary was recorded as a widow and mother of one child. Although her parents were alive and she was in regular contact with them, she listed her son Richard Bradley as her next of kin, stating that he was at the Dr Barnardo's Home, Stephen Causeway. She wrote to her mother when she was allowed and family members visited when visits were permitted. In October 1884 she was moved to Woking Prison and worked as a tailor. She committed only one offence against the rules in prison; she was caught laughing during a school examination and was rude when checked by the prison officer. For this indiscipline she was placed in separation in the penal ward for seven days and lost twelve remission marks. In November 1886 Mary was given a conditional licence, just over halfway through her sentence, and was sent to Russell House Refuge. Her release was permitted by the Directors of Convict Prisons nine months later. By 1891 her father had died, and she was living with her mother and brother in Tottenham; and working as a charwoman.

58. Elizabeth Jones (born 1813, near Yeovil, Somerset) Licence no. A37717/ 7484

Arson was the 'malicious and wilful burning of a house or outhouse of another man' (Blackstone, 1769). It was often employed by those taking vengeance against victims and could be highly destructive, especially in rural areas, where fires were in remote locations and fire services limited. Arson could also be a form of social protest against low wages, unemployment or other grievances and in these cases might have wider support in the local community. The expansion of insurance companies also increased the attempts to defraud as well as the degree to which fires were investigated. Arson was a capital offence until 1837 demonstrating the seriousness with which the offence was viewed.

Victorian firemen (*Henry Mayhew*, London Labour and London Poor, *vol. III, 1861*)

Elizabeth Jones and her husband John were accused of setting fire to a dwelling house with the intention of defrauding the insurance company in the summer of 1883. At the time of the fire one of the lodgers was also asleep in the building. Elizabeth was nearly 70 years old and John was about six years older. For both of the accused, it was their first and only offence.

The couple kept a beershop and lodging house (Sidney's Inn in Sidford Street, Millbrook, Southampton) and had done for at least the previous thirteen years. On the day of the fire, Arthur Blake had noticed the flames and smoke coming from the upstairs window at about 11 o'clock. He entered the house to find Elizabeth at the top of the stairs and he said he could put the fire out but she prevented him by pushing him down the stairs. A man named Samuel Webber burst the door open when the police arrived and by this time the bedstead was red hot, the fire in the centre of the bed. Both of the prisoners had been turning people away from the house and would not let any water inside. Elizabeth had stated that Mr Guy, one of their lodgers, was asleep in the house. Webber kicked the door open, finding Guy asleep with smoke, but not fire, in the room. It was claimed that there were perhaps a dozen or eighteen people or more gathered outside the house with buckets of water but the prisoners refused to let them use it. Another witness corroborated the evidence and said that the fire smelt like burnt feathers and paraffin and there was a box containing rags soaked with paraffin or other oil as well as boxes with rubbish for the fire. When searched by the police, Elizabeth had seven pounds and eight shillings on her and John had three coats, a number of razors and other articles in his possession. They also found boxes and baskets tied up with string, ready for removal and an insurance policy with the Caledonian Insurance Company for £100, dated 5 February 1878. At Hampshire Assizes, the judge remarked that they were guilty of 'a very heinous offence ... and great carelessness with regard to the life of the old man who had been your lodger for so many years'. He sentenced them to seven years' penal servitude.

In prison, both were placed in Star Class as first offenders. Elizabeth wrote from Millbank to Pentonville to find out about her husband's health, who was said to be 'feeble and infirm due to age', but not suffering. She also spent time in the infirmary due to old age, infirmity and falling from a hammock; and she was deaf. John died either in prison or shortly after release. Elizabeth was released on licence in July 1886 and was escorted to her brother's house; and by 1891 she was living alone at 7 Regent Street, Millbrook supported by her brother.

59. Mary Jones (born 1839 Hambledon, Surrey) Licence no. 3536

Brixton Prison ironing room (*H. Mayhew and J. Binny*, The Criminal Prisons of London and Scenes of London Life, *1862*)

Infanticide is the murder of an infant child by its mother. The crime was first defined in an Act of 1624 but in the eighteenth century the conviction rate fell and by 1803 the Act was repealed and a new offence of 'concealment of birth' was created. Under this women could prove that they had prepared for the birth and had not intended to murder their child. After 1849 no-one was hanged for murdering their baby, though they might originally have been sentenced to death. In 1922 the Infanticide Act created the new offence of infanticide of a newly born child whilst the balance of the mother's mind was disturbed. The subsequent Infanticide Act (1938) amended this to within one year of birth and offered different defences to the offence.

Nineteen-year-old Mary Jones, an unmarried servant from Hambledon in Surrey, was sentenced to death for the wilful murder of her illegitimate female child in March 1859. The trial was unusual as there were no counsel for the prosecution or for the defence. The *Hampshire Advertiser* commented that the prisoner was 'in an almost fainting state during the trial, and appeared to be hardly conscious of what was going on' (2 April, 1859). Mary had been seduced and found herself pregnant; the pregnancy was suspected by a number of people but she had always denied this was the case. She was taken ill on 27 August, her neighbour made some mint tea for her and upon entering the bedroom immediately suspected she had given birth. Blood was seen coming from a box near the bedside and a blood-soaked knife lay on the floor. A full-grown female baby was discovered in the box, its throat had been cut and everything was saturated in blood. Mr Chandler, a surgeon, examined the body, finding the throat cut to be so severe that death had been instantaneous. He thought that the child had been born alive and had died as a result of the wound.

Mary admitted in court that the baby was hers and said she used the knife to cut the umbilical cord; and that she had placed the child in the box as she did not know what else to do with it. She sobbed, said she was in agony and had not known what she was doing. The jury found her guilty of wilful murder, though strongly recommended her to mercy. The judge, Mr Baron Martin, put on the black cap and passed sentence, whereupon Mary fainted and was carried from the court. He said: 'I hoped that her unfortunate example will be a warning to other young women, and that if they sinned in the manner she had done they would learn that the proper course was for them to communicate with their friends and inform them of their condition, and not endeavour to conceal their shame by an act of this dreadful character'.

The judge had summed up the case, leaning towards the lesser charge of concealment of birth but the jury had disagreed. The judge wrote immediately to the Home Secretary stating that death should not be inflicted in this case. The *Daily News* said the act had taken place 'during the agony of a first confinement, aggravated by the misery and distress of the position in which she was placed and that there was nothing whatever to show that she had any deliberate intention to destroy the life of her offspring' (7 April, 1859). Mary had been committed to Horsemonger Lane Gaol to await execution, but her sentence was later commuted to penal servitude for life. She served over nine years in Brixton Prison, and a short time in Woking Prison, and was released on licence on 12 April 1870.

60. Bridget Kelly (born 1862, Chatham, Kent) Licence no. 7487

Clerkenwell Prison at visiting time
(*H. Mayhew and J. Binny*, The
Criminal Prisons of London and
Scenes of London Life, *1862*)

On the site of former carceral institutions, Clerkenwell House of Detention (also known as Middlesex House of Detention) was opened in 1847. Many prisoners like Bridget Kelly were kept there until their trial was held. One man, an Irish nationalist, was exercising in the yard when his comrades attempted to blow down the walls to help him escape in 1867. The explosion was so powerful that 12 people were killed and 120 bystanders outside the prison were injured. The ringleader of the escape attempt was caught, and became the last man to be publically executed outside of Newgate Prison. Clerkenwell Prison was closed in 1890.

Born to Irish parents in Chatham, Kent, Bridget grew up with her parents and siblings in one of the poorer parts of London. Whitecross Street, St Lukes, was situated near Islington and her parents may have worked at the nearby market (nicknamed Squalor's Market). With her eighteenth birthday passed, Bridget seems to have launched into a series of minor offences in the local area (being dealt with at Worship Street, and at Thames police courts). In January 1889, she was convicted of drunkenness (seven days' gaol); the following month she was riotous and served another seven days; in April, disorderliness earned her yet another seven days, and an assault got her two more months; and in November and December another two assaults earned her fourteen days, and one month's gaol sentence respectively. The following year followed a similar pattern (her most serious offence being the convictions in October at Middlesex Sessions for theft and wounding, which saw her receive two years in gaol).

Almost exactly twelve months later she was convicted at the Old Bailey of stealing a purse containing £4 and she started five years' penal servitude after awaiting her trial in Clerkenwell House of Detention. In convict prison she was punished for fighting, and other breaches of prison rules, including 'having a fire in her cell during the dinner hour'. Almost as soon as she was allowed to go to the refuge at East End House, Finchley, she was recalled to Fulham Prison. Her prison file records the reason: leaving her work in the Refuge laundry, and being insubordinate to the Matron. Once back in Fulham she was disciplined for 'striking AJ153 McCarthy a blow on her face, holding her head down on the ironing table threatening her, also kicking her in a most savage manner causing a great disturbance in no. 1 laundry'. In 1886 she requested that she be sent to the Discharged Prisoners' Aid Society (DPAS) before emigrating abroad.

In this period many Irish-born workers, and others who wanted to try their luck in a new land, were travelling across the Atlantic to America. Many ex-convicts were also facilitated to start a new life overseas. The DPAS were willing to help, and they replied that if she was 'at this office by 12 o'clock noon on 2 Sept 1886 she will be in for emigrating the same afternoon'. However, the prison would not allow this, and her emigration order was cancelled.

On 2 September 1886, Bridget was released on licence with thirteen months of her sentence left to serve. The note on her file said that she was due to emigrate, and perhaps she did journey on to a new country and a new life, for Bridget never re-appeared in criminal records after her release.

61. Catherine Kendall (born c.1843, Ireland) Licence no. 79356

Mary Ann Cotton, She's dead and she's rotten,
She lies in her bed, With eyes wide open.
Sing, sing, oh, what can I sing,
Mary Ann Cotton is tied up with string.

Where, where?, Up in the air,
Sellin' black puddings a penny a pair.
Mary Ann Cotton, She's dead and forgotten,
She lies in a grave with her bones all-rotten;
Sing, sing, oh, what can we sing,
Mary Ann Cotton is tied up with string.

(*Contemporary doggerel verse about Mary Ann Cotton*)

Catherine Kendall (née Curley) was born in Ireland around 1843. By 1851 (possibly as a result of the Great Potato Famine) her family had moved to England and in 1851 were living in Hartlepool; her father Patrick being a dock labourer. Ten years later, Catherine married Henry Kendall (also a dock labourer) at Hartlepool and the couple continued to live with her parents and family. By 1871, Catherine and Henry had moved to Jarrow, where Henry found work as a labourer. They eventually had at least four children (Henry, Thomas, Mary and Frances).

Durham Prison (where Catherine spent time in both 1874 and 1881, awaiting transfer to convict prison) dates back to 1809. On 31 July of that year the foundation stone was laid, but it was not until ten years later that the prison was ready to receive its first contingent of prisoners. Almost 100 individuals were executed in the prison over a period of 150 years, and its gallows were last used in 1958. By far the most famous individual to be hanged there was Mary Ann Cotton (1832-73), who was found guilty of poisoning her fourth husband, Frederick (to whom she was actually married bigamously) with arsenic. She was also suspected of (but never tried for) the murder of up to fifteen of her relatives by the same method in order to claim their life insurance policies.

The following year, Catherine made her first recorded appearance in court, charged with stealing cloth in Jarrow. She was sentenced to one month's imprisonment. Over the next three years her petty offending continued, with several convictions for theft of clothes and bedding (possibly suggesting that she and Henry had fallen on hard times). In January 1875 she was found guilty of the theft of two jackets and a piece of wool at Durham Sessions and sentenced to seven years' penal servitude. The majority of her sentence was served at Millbank in London, and this obviously restricted her access to visits by her family; she wrote to her husband on numerous occasions, but did not receive any reply.

On 29 March 1876 Catherine petitioned the governor of Millbank to find out any news of her husband, but was told that there was no word from him. She also complained that she was not receiving any letters from her friends or family, despite writing to them.

On 24 December 1878 she received a conditional licence after serving four years of her sentence. She first goes to the East End Refuge and then returns to Jarrow. In the first quarter of 1881 Henry died. Catherine offended once more; stealing a skirt, and received a second sentence of seven years' penal servitude at Durham Sessions. She is recorded in the 1881 census as a widowed white-lead factory worker and a prisoner at Durham Prison. She is sent once again to Millbank, before being transferred in late-1881 to Woking. During her time at Millbank she sent and received correspondence from a James Carney, c/o Mr Palmer, Iron shipyard, Jarrow. Police enquiries stated that Catherine had been cohabiting with Palmer, and that Carney was a known Home Rule supporter, but that nothing was known against him.

Catherine appears to have been reconciled with her children following the death of her husband and maintained a regular correspondence with both her eldest son and daughter, as well as with James Carney throughout the remainder of her sentence. She was released once more on licence in December 1886 and went to live with her married daughter Elizabeth in Southampton. She died in late-1911 in Hartlepool.

62. Robert Kidd (born 1831, Westminster, London) Licence no. 124555

Robert spent many years in Wandsworth Prison. Originally the site of Surrey House of Corrections, the prison was built in 1851 on a 26-acre site (it is still one of the largest prisons in Europe). It was designed according to the separate system principle with 700 prisoners held in individual cells. The main part of the prison was reserved for male prisoners with a smaller separate building for females, and two further wings were added in 1856. When Horsemonger Lane Gaol was closed in 1878, executions were subsequently transferred to Wandsworth Prison, and the prison saw 134 men and one woman hanged there between 1878 and 1961.

Robert Kidd, aged 43
(*The National Archives*)

Robert Kidd first appeared before the Surrey Quarter Sessions in 1851 when he was sentenced to four months in gaol for stealing a navigable boat. By his mid-twenties Robert was a potter's labourer; he was single; he could read and write; and he belonged to the Church of England. He may have been in the Navy as he had a sailor and flag and anchors tattooed on his wrists; and he had previous convictions 'in the East'. By 1852 Robert had lost part of his left leg due to 'white swelling' or scrofula (a tumour of the joint; which was usually treated by amputation).

He received his first sentence of penal servitude in 1862 when Surrey Sessions found him guilty of stealing a pair of slippers and sentenced him to four years. Robert was then sent to Millbank. There, all convicts underwent a period of separate confinement: working, sleeping and eating in their solitary cell. They only left the cell for exercise (during which they would be masked) and to attend chapel, and no communication was permitted. On completion, convicts were sent to public works prisons and due to his disability, in 1862, Robert was moved to Woking Invalid Prison. He was released from prison ten months early with licence conditions, which he then broke by failing to report to the police on a regular basis. Consequently, he was returned to prison and subsequently released at the end of his sentence in March 1866.

The following year Robert received ten years' penal servitude for the theft of a pair of trousers. In prison he complained about his treatment by the Medical Officer on a number of occasions. The Medical Officer countered that Robert was 'an old person and seems desirous of spending his time in hospital'. Disagreements continued until July 1876 when Robert was 45 years old and he was released again on licence with fifteen months of his sentence unserved.

In August 1879, Robert then received another ten years for larceny. His petitions to the Secretary of State pleading for mitigation of his sentence were refused. In 1880 he transferred to Parkhurst Prison on the Isle of Wight where he spent the next seven years. Robert once again spent time under the care of the Medical Officer, suffering from eczema, then bronchitis, and he also got in trouble for avoiding three hours' labour by sending in a sick note after he had just been treated. By February 1887 he was declared unfit for labour of any kind and was permitted to grow his hair in preparation for release on licence. He was given clothing in which to be discharged, and a crutch; and his leg was bandaged when he was released on licence on 24 May 1887, two years and four months early. From the records available, Robert committed no further crimes and on the 1891 Census he was simply described as a 60-year-old retired potter living in the Newington Workhouse, St Saviour's Union. Robert died there a year later.

63. **Catherine Lindsay** (born 1843, Liverpool) Licence no. A25906/ 7563

A range of punishments was used against prisoners such as Catherine when they had broken prison rules and regulations. The progressive stage system allowed for stage marks and marks for remission to be taken away, this meant that prisoners had to serve more time at an earlier stage or that they would lose days off their sentence thus not getting out as early as they otherwise might. Prisoners were admonished, they were placed in close confinement or in penal class or their diet might be restricted or they were given a bread and water diet, or they may receive a combination of these punishments. Prisoners might also be placed in a canvas dress or in a straitjacket and in severe cases, men could be flogged.

Catherine Lindsay, aged c.40
(*The National Archives*)

Catherine Lindsay aka Margaret O'Donnell or Margaret Heart, Margaret Burns, Margaret Lindsay, Catherine Gordon, Catherine Riley, Catherine McDonnell spent over three decades incarcerated in various prisons. After a couple of short prison sentences for petty crimes, she was sent to a juvenile reformatory for five years for 'not being able to account for money'. Aged thirteen or fourteen, she had been born in either Dublin or Liverpool in the early 1840s. Catherine served some huge periods of time in prison, mainly for theft.

A year after her release, she was convicted of stealing a watch and received eight years' penal servitude, a hefty sentence, even by the standards of the day. Catherine found imprisonment difficult and committed a huge number of prison offences against rules, sixty-seven offences (such as kicking her cell door, singing, shouting, insolence and destroying prison property). She was released on licence in November 1868, but this was revoked due to 'habitually associating with bad characters'. She committed another seventeen offences before she had served all of her prison sentence and was released. About seven weeks later, she received three months' imprisonment for stealing a gold ring. In August 1874, she was sentenced to seven years' penal servitude for stealing a watch.

Back in prison her offences against the rules continued, though she committed only nine before she was released on conditional licence to the East End Refuge, thirty-four months early. Catherine was returned from the Refuge after she violently attacked another prisoner. She was granted another licence in November 1879 and headed back to Liverpool. In January 1880 she was charged with not informing the police of a change of address and her licence was again revoked. Catherine committed another five prison offences and was twice placed in a canvas dress. In August 1881 she was released again but by February 1882 was back in court; she received another five years' penal servitude for stealing a watch. Her physical and mental health also began to suffer after years of institutionalisation. She committed four more prison offences and attempted suicide, though she was not punished for this as it was regarded as genuine. She was released on licence in July 1885, but after being found in unlawful possession of a watch and her licence was revoked in November. She petitioned the Secretary of State, he said if she stayed sane and behaved he would consider her case in twelve months or she would be removed to a criminal lunatic asylum with indefinite date of release. The medical officer acknowledged her depression and proneness to suicide. Finally, she was released on special licence in December 1886, and perhaps unsurprisingly there is no further trace of her in the records.

64. Lucy Lowe (born 1841, Stagsden, Lincolnshire) Licence no. 56783/7506

Bust of John Howard
(*Authors' Collections*)

Bedford Prison is probably most famous due to the Sheriff of Bedford, John Howard (see image) who, in the late-eighteenth century led the nationwide prison reform movement, and published *The State of the Prisons* in 1777. A new gaol was built in 1801 and in 1819 a house of correction was built next door, in 1854, the two institutions were merged. The prison was retained when the local prisons were centralised under the Prison Commission. You can search the Bedfordshire Gaol Registers through an online database at http://apps.bedfordshire.gov.uk/grd/ (currently it covers the period from 1801 to 1879). HMP Bedford still operates as a Category B local prison today and holds around 500 male prisoners.

Lucy Riddy was born in Stagsden, Bedford in 1841, she grew up in the same area and when she was about 20 years old married Samuel Ellis. Within a year, Lucy was a widow with a small baby and was living with her parents. Four years later, she married Ellis Lowe and in the following years, they had four daughters. In March 1876 she was charged with the wilful murder of a female child of twenty-one days. Lucy had been arrested at the home of Reverend W. Kirkham of Hampstead, where she had been working as a domestic servant. It was claimed that Lucy had suffocated the child and thrown the body into a plantation, near Turvey in Bedfordshire. The body had been found by a gamekeeper who said that the bag had been tied up tight over the child's head and around the neck and this had caused the suffocation. Lucy had told a witness who had seen her with the child, that the child was being cared for by her sister in Derby. During the trial it was noted that Lucy's second husband had left in 1873 and the children had been placed in the workhouse. In her defence it was claimed that the child had suffered from fits; these were observed by a witness, and that the child had died and Lucy had panicked and left the body. The claims were to no avail as the jury found her guilty of wilful murder and she was sentenced to death.

Lucy was committed to Bedford Prison to await execution on 24 July at 8.00am. In the condemned cell she was under constant observation from the staff. But her execution was not carried out as the Home Secretary ordered that the death sentence be commuted to penal servitude for life. Lucy was received at Millbank in August and then the following April was moved to Woking Prison where she undertook needlework and mosaic tiling. Throughout her imprisonment she wrote to her parents and siblings; and her parents also visited when regulations permitted. In 1881 three of her daughters were still in Bedford Union Workhouse. In 1882 her father passed away and in 1883 two of her daughters, Ada and Harriet died.

After nine years in prison Lucy petitioned the Home Secretary for remission of her sentence, admitting that the crime had occurred in an hour of 'despair, grief and madness'. A second petition followed eight months later, stating that her sister would receive her and that she had been driven to the crime by 'excessive grief, shame and despair'. By June 1886 Lucy had served ten years in prison, she had no previous convictions, her conduct and industry in prison had been very good, she was admonished only once during her imprisonment, for talking loudly. In August 1886 she was granted a licence to be at large and she was released on 3 September of that year.

65. William MacAdam (born 1829, Glasgow) Licence 67320/45505

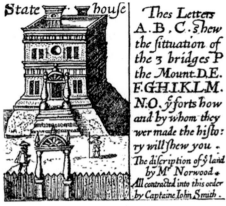

Bermuda Convict establishment
(*Authors' Collections*)

Criminologists today talk of the prison 'churn' – the movement of prisoners around the prison system. Churning is thought by the authorities to prevent long-term relationships and friendships forming between prisoners, or between prisoners and prison staff, thereby lessening the danger of collusion and corruption. The experience of William Macadam shows that the churn was also part of the Victorian prison system. MacAdam even experienced foreign penal institutions such as Boaz Island, Bermuda, part of the same system of penal transportation as the convicts in Australia, Singapore, the Andaman Islands, and Gibraltar.

Born in 1829 in Glasgow, William was first convicted in Liverpool, aged 29, as a married man with one child, working as a 'commission agent'. He was found guilty of gaining surgical instruments by 'false pretences' and sentenced to seven years' penal servitude. Although transportation was winding down in this period, William's penal experience still took him around the world. He was first taken to the *Tenados* prison ship where he spent nine months. He was stationed at the Boaz Prison Island Penal Colony, Bermuda, for the next two years, carrying out hard labour, before returning to Millbank, and being released from his sentence.

In 1869 he was convicted of false pretences again in Liverpool, and served eighteen months in custody, also within a period of four months in 1872–73 he was found not guilty of forgery, and of stealing a watch. His luck ran out when he tried his fortune across the water in Ireland, being convicted of fraud at Dublin Sessions and receiving five years in the Irish penal system. Three months after being released from Mountjoy Prison in 1877 he was sentenced to five years at Liverpool, yet again for false pretences. His wife was now refusing to return his letters from prison (she would die in 1887), and his daughter had emigrated to Canada.

He was released on licence on 31 August 1881, and re-convicted on 23 May 1882 of false pretences at Preston sessions. The local newspaper recorded that he was 'a shabby broken down fellow... more than a third of his life had been spent in gaol'. He served four more years in prison, before being released a year early on licence. He died in 1897, aged 67, in Liverpool.

During his various sentences, William spent time in prisons in Liverpool, Wakefield, Chatham, Millbank, Pentonville, Portsmouth, Preston, Parkhurst and Borstal; as well as Boaz Island, Bermuda. Not so much a career criminal as a career prisoner, he spent the first half of his life gaining a respectable position, a wife, a child, and the beginnings of a successful life. He then appears to have changed direction completely, learning how to gain property and money through false pretences, forgery, and fraud. He then spends much of the rest of his life in various institutions, losing his family and respectability along the way. We will never know whether it was financial pressure – the threat of losing his job perhaps – or a personal problem, love of gambling or alcohol, or some such individual failing, that propelled him into a life of crime. Whatever the reason, his decision to falsely acquire those surgical instruments in 1857 changed the direction of his life dramatically, and for the worse.

66. Rhodes Marriott (born 1821, Ashover, Derbyshire) Medical Discharge

Dartmoor Prison in 1879
(*Authors' Collections*)

Dartmoor was originally constructed to hold thousands of French and American prisoners of war in the early nineteenth century. The prison was empty for a number of decades until it was re-opened in the 1850s to hold convicts. The prison on the moors has always captured popular imagination, and it has featured in many works of literature. Dartmoor was used to hold conscientious objectors to World War I, but was again open to (sometimes very famous) convicts from 1920. The prison increased its fame as a result of events such as the 1932 prison mutiny which was the most serious disturbance in modern times.

In his early twenties, Rhodes Marriott married Mary Morton at St Peter and St Paul Church, Eckington, Derbyshire, in 1843. This was a very difficult economic period, and it would have been difficult for Rhodes and his new bride to find secure employment. Perhaps that explains the reasons why he was convicted of theft on 19 November 1849. After release from Derby Prison, where he served six months, his life took a serious turn, when he and his father were placed on trial for sheep-stealing at Derby Assizes. On 20 March 1850 his father was acquitted, but Rhodes was sentenced to seven years transportation. Had he actually sailed to Australia, both his and his wife's lives would have been vastly affected. As it was, like many convicts at this time, he spent some time on a hulk before being deposited in the newly re-opened Dartmoor Prison.

Three years later, on 24 October 1853, he was discharged on medical grounds with almost three and a half years of his sentence still to serve. As he was halfway through his sentence, he may have been due for early release on licence anyway, but we lack information as to why he was discharged rather than licensed. Many prisoners requested mitigation or reduction of their sentences because they were ill, but very few requests were ever granted. Frustratingly, the information on his prison record reveals very little of the reasons why his particular request was granted. It certainly was not because of a terminal illness, for, as future censuses testify, he lived for a long time after leaving Dartmoor.

In 1851 and 1861, the censuses record him as living with his wife Mary back in Eckington. Rhodes was then working as a coalminer, as was his 15-year-old son. Mary had given birth to another son in 1857, and the marriage seems to have been a happy one since they lived together for many years. Rhodes seemed settled after his one term of penal servitude. He seems to have had a poetic turn of mind, writing several verses about his birthplace of Ashover; and in 1891 a newspaper reported that Rhodes had been made President of the Hornthorpes branch (Eckington) of the Miners' Permanent Relief Fund.

A few years later, his wife died, and tragically his son Samuel was killed in a mining accident at Renishaw Park Colliery in 1909 when he was crushed to death when the shaft he was working in collapsed. A detailed account of the tragedy can be found online at http://www.healeyhero.co.uk/rescue/pits/Renshaw/Renshaw2.htm.

Rhodes died in the autumn of 1911 in Chesterfield registration district.

67. John McSally (born c.1850, Gateshead) Licence no. A6108/45202

A ward on the *Unite* Hospital Ship (*H. Mayhew and J. Binny*, The Criminal Prisons of London and Scenes of London Life, *1862*)

Convict prisons and hulks were equipped with infirmaries in order to treat sick convicts within a secure environment. The general standard of health of many offenders entering convict prisons was poor. All convicts had their health assessed at the time of entry to the prison, and if, as in the case with McSally, they had an existing chronic condition, they would often be sent straight to the infirmary. Occasionally the incurable nature of the convict's illness could lead them to be released early on licence. One of the most prevalent conditions seen in new entries to the prison was venereal disease. Convicts who had earned the trust of the prison officials were often employed as attendants to nurse their sickly inmates.

For an unknown reason John is not registered as living with his family in the 1861 census, and in the following census of 1871 he is living with his maternal uncle Robert Dawson, a fruiterer in North Shields. His first record offence took place in January 1873, when he was found guilty of larceny and sentenced to two months' imprisonment at North Shields. In April 1881 he was found guilty of shop-breaking at Newcastle Assizes. He and his accomplice, Joseph Murray, were described by the judge as 'a black as pair of rascals as one might wish to see'.

He was sentenced to seven years' penal servitude, and entered Pentonville Prison in May of that year. However, upon medical examination he was found to be suffering from chronic bronchitis and was excused hard labour, instead being sent directly to the prison infirmary. Five days later he was transferred to Millbank Prison infirmary, where he remained until 1 July. He was readmitted to the infirmary on 19 August and remained there until he was transferred once again, this time to Woking Prison (where chronic cases usually ended up, as it had a large infirmary within its confines). He was diagnosed with phthisis.

He petitioned the Secretary of State on 22 April 1882 and again during the following year, but with no success. He continued to enter petitions throughout the rest of his sentence, but was unsuccessful despite the

Medical Officer originally stating that in his opinion, McSally was currently 'in hospital suffering from pulmonary consumption, thus is a permanent invalid requiring constant medical attention, careful nursing, and that he is in my opinion totally and permanently unfit for prison discipline. He is fit for removal to his home in Durham'. In the second of his reports on McSally's health, the Medical Officer appears to have changed his mind somewhat – he stated that 'the phthisis was a pre-existing condition that was not necessarily exacerbated by prison life', further remarking that 'his health will probably be prolonged by imprisonment considering the probable conditions of life to which he would be subjected if released'.

McSalley clearly maintained contact with the area of his birth. He kept in touch with both his uncle Robert Dawson (who wrote him numerous letters throughout the period of his imprisonment) and with another uncle, Thomas Havron. No letters appear to have been either written to, or received from either of his parents). Despite being unsuccessful with his numerous petitions, McSalley did eventually gain early release on licence on 22 February 1887, having served five years and ten months of his seven-year sentence. He was released to St Giles Mission, but no further trace of his life can be found.

68. William James Milson (born 1822, Shoreditch, London) Licence no. 331

Bethlehem Asylum (*Public Domain*)

Bethlehem Hospital had its origins in the thirteenth century, though it became associated with treating mental illness a century later. Ex-patients were referred to as 'Bedlamites' and given permission to beg on main routes between towns. Into the 1800s it was the only public institution for mental health. In 1676 it moved to Moorfields and its high profile and inquiries into abuse of patients lead to reforms but also associated the term 'Bedlam' with unruly situations. The hospital relocated again in 1815 for more space indoors and outdoors seen central to the moral treatment of patients. In 1930 it moved to Beckenham, London and today Bethlem Royal Hospital is a research and treatment centre.

William James Milson was apparently a well-educated husband and father of three when he was convicted at the Central Criminal Court for obtaining money by false pretences and sentenced to seven years' transportation. The trial had revealed a different side to Milson and his many identities. Milson had a number of aliases: Charles Chadwick, an architect; Dr James William Harris, a surgeon; William Williams and William Baillie, a solicitor. The charges that were initially bought by the father of a young man, Benjamin Thomas Hartrop, who had been working in the architect's office, his father having paid in a sum in advance for his training. The agreement was that Benjamin be apprenticed to Chadwick, who also presented himself as a Quaker, for three years. The son started work in August and then went into the office on 10th November to find the buildings shut up. In giving evidence, Benjamin said there were eight other persons in the office, like himself, though there was no real business.

The prosecution had brought forward other interested parties, as the following witness stated that he had rented a house to Milson, who also claimed to be a former candidate for St Albans, but some time later a sign appeared on the door saying 'Dr Harris'. The witness went to the house after the prisoner had removed all of the furniture and challenged Milson about the rent, the defendant allegedly threatened the witness.

Further witnesses stated that they or family members had been medically treated by the defendant and a young man, Bellares, under his supervision. In one instance, a baby had died of whooping cough and the death certificate had been signed by the defendant. Mr Vann, for the prosecution, stated he had evidence for at least twenty cases against Milson. On discovery of the frauds, Milson had begged one witness not to take him into custody and claimed he had acted only out of distress; he then offered the witness twelve shillings not to press charges.

Milson was found guilty and sentenced to seven years transportation. The *Morning Post* stated that he 'seemed quite unprepared for the sentence, and taking up his hat with one hand covered his face with the other, and walked slowly from the dock' (20 December 1851).

Milson was committed to Newgate Prison in December 1851 and then in January moved to Millbank; and after eleven months in separate confinement there he was moved to the public works at Portsmouth prison. In March 1853 he was removed to Bethlehem Hospital after being declared insane but was returned to Portsmouth Prison in October of the same year. In December 1853 he received his licence, with five years unserved, and gave his father's address in Old Kent Road.

69. John Minto (born c.1847, Newcastle Upon Tyne) Licence no. A20227

Flogging 'A' frame
(*Authors' Collections*)

John Minto was by no means a model prisoner during any of his numerous stretches in prison. He was often insolent and insubordinate to warders and fought with other prisoners on several occasions. As a result he received the full gamut of punishments that could be awarded to him by the prison governor. He forfeited many remission marks, was put on a reduced diet, was kept in close confinement for periods, and also had his mattress taken away on at least one occasion. The most serious penalty for infringements of discipline was corporal punishment in the form of a flogging with the 'cat o'nine tails'. In 1883 Minto struck a prison warder and was sentenced to 'receive corporal punishment of 24 lashes with the cat in the authorised manner without unnecessary delay'. This sentence would have been administered in the prison exercise yard with Minto strapped to an 'A' frame.

John Minto's offending life began at an early age; he was convicted at the age of 16 of public gaming in the street (probably some form of pitch and toss, a game of chance which involved betting on how close a thrown stone could get to the edge of a wall), and sentenced to fourteen days' imprisonment. This was the start of a number of appearances before Bradford magistrates, and he soon displayed violent tendencies, being convicted of assault on five occasions over a period of two years. However, his offending escalated; in November 1867 he was accused of stealing a watch 'in a most daring manner from Mr William Bickley Beaney, while the prosecutor was proceeding along Leeds Road, Bradford, shortly after midnight'. The *Leeds Mercury* further described him as 'an old offender'. He was found guilty and sentenced to five years' penal servitude. Whilst at Portsmouth Prison he fought with another prisoner, was insolent to a prison warder, and 'used his urinal for an improper purpose'. For these offences he lost many remission marks and was kept in close confinement for a number of days. On 4 March 1870 he was found guilty of 'idleness and using insubordinate and disgusting language and repeating some of it before the governor'. Despite such bad behaviour, on 5 January 1872 he was released on licence, with almost a year of his sentence unserved.

Convict prison did not reform him; in August 1873 Minto was returned to prison, having been found guilty of stealing a box of mason's tools, valued at 50 shillings. He was sentenced to seven years' penal servitude, to be followed by five years' police supervision. He stayed in touch both with his wife and parents throughout his regular stints inside. On 28 June 1879 he was again released on licence, and returned to Bradford. Within four months his licence had been revoked as he had been caught using obscene language and he was returned to Pentonville. He was released on 19 January 1881, but in April 1881 was found guilty of attempted breaking and entering of a warehouse; he was caught red-handed, being found impaled through his leg on the iron spikes of a gateway leading to the warehouse. He stated in court that he had slipped on top of the gate whilst trying to recover an errant hat of his that had been thrown over the gate. He was sentenced to one month's imprisonment. Having served this, he came out and on 27 June 1881 and was sentenced to another seven years' penal servitude and five years' police supervision. Despite attacking a warder and being flogged and shackled whilst at Borstal Prison, he was again released on licence on 15 March 1887. In 1896 he was sentenced to six months at Bradford for warehouse-breaking.

John Minto then appears to have stopped offending, possibly due to his leg injury, working as a plasterer and living for many years with his wife Anne in Bradford, until she died in 1909. He spent some time in Bradford Union Workhouse and died at the age of 77 in 1924.

70. Julia Murray (born 1827, Cork, Ireland) Licence no. 3720

Liverpool's old prison in the centre of the city was replaced by Walton Prison in 1855. Designed to hold a thousand inmates it became an important institution in a developing city booming with American trade. Julia was by no means the most famous of its inmates, which included, for example, Fenner Brockway, the conscientious objector and Labour MP. The prison was badly bombed during World War Two, with sixty-two inmates killed in one raid (the prisoners had not been evacuated by the authorities). The prison is still in service today, although it has now been renamed HMP Liverpool.

Fenner Brockway (1888–1988)
(*Public Domain*)

In June 1854 a newspaper report stated that 'Julia Murray, a deaf and dumb young woman, who earns her livelihood by hawking oysters, was charged at the Manchester police court with stabbing a man named Thomas Taylor with an oyster knife ...the prisoner, by signs, denied that she stabbed the man. She was discharged, after receiving a caution by the bench'. Thomas had approached Julia when he was intoxicated, and, not being able to shout at him to leave her alone, they had struggled. When Thomas fell to the ground, he got up with a wound to his body caused by Julia's oyster knife. As she had no previous convictions, the court may have given her the benefit of the doubt. Julia then avoided trouble until 1861 when she was convicted of stealing money in Liverpool and given a three-month gaol sentence. Nine months gaol sentence for a similar offence followed almost as soon as she had been released from Walton Prison. She may again have had a little fortune when she was found not guilty of stealing money at Liverpool in May 1863. Her luck ran out, however, when she was sentenced in 1866 to seven years' penal servitude by Liverpool Borough Sessions for the offence of larceny from the person.

When she was in convict prison she was punished for 'making signs to her officer signifying that if her brother came to see her and left some money for her officer, she would always be good to her'. Given that charge, it seems odd that there was still some doubt that Julia was deaf and dumb-born. In August

1868 the Governor of Liverpool Walton Prison wrote to the Governor of Parkhurst to inform him that 'it was never doubted here that convict Julia Young was not deaf and dumb-born. She was always so during her frequent and long imprisonments here, and when visited periodically by her friends always communicated with them by signs only'. Julia served her time in prison with only a few breaches of prison rules, and she was released on licence on 13 December 1870 via Eagle House Refuge. She did not indicate her intended place of abode when she left prison.

Julia did not appear in criminal registers after her penal servitude. Did she stop offending? There are two possibilities; on 5 September 1871 a Julia Murrey, aged 44, born in Ireland, sailed for New York from Liverpool. Had Julia sailed for the New World, or did Julia drift into poverty and end up in the workhouse? The 1881 census records a Julia Murray, aged 55, born in Cork, Ireland, as an inmate in Whitechapel Workhouse, London. Were either of these women the Julia Murray who had ended up in convict prison some years earlier? We will never know.

71. Mary Ann Murray (born 1856, Lambeth) Licence no. 57855/7527

final disposal.

Mary's daughter, Mary Ellen, was housed in an industrial school opened by The Sisters of Mercy in 1874. She may have moved along with the other children when the Industrial School was relocated to larger premises at Croydon in 1887. If she did, it was only for a year as the School moved back to Eltham the following year. The industrial school system took in children who were not convicted of any crime themselves, but were at risk of falling into a criminal career, or who had no-one to look after them (through being 'beyond parental control'); by being orphaned or abandoned; or, as was the case here, when the child's parents were in prison'.

Mary Ann Murray aged 21
(*The National Archives*)

From the age of 14, Mary had been in and out of the London courts. After serving two short sentences, she was convicted at Surrey Sessions of stealing a purse containing over £9. In 1874 Mary and an accomplice had invited some sailors who were moored in London to come and share drinks with them in a public house. One of the sailors was drugged by the women, and his money taken. The arresting police constable gave evidence that the women were well known in the neighbourhood for this daring kind of offence, but that other victims had been too drunk, drugged, or embarrassed to give proper evidence in court. This time the sailors and the police officer convinced the court that the women were accomplished robbers, and at the age of 18, she was received five years' penal servitude; and started her sentence in Millbank's separate and silent system.

In 1876 she petitioned to go to a refuge having less than nine months sentence left to serve. She was licensed to Battery House Refuge with twenty-nine months unserved, and in May 1876, the Directors give her permission to leave the refuge. Mary had clearly had a difficult start to life, and she was not able to take advantage of her freedom to begin over again, despite having had a child in the brief period she was free. After being out of prison for less than a year she was convicted of stealing from a person again and sentenced to ten years' penal servitude at Surrey Sessions.

In her first penal servitude she had obeyed the prison rules, by and large, with only two breaches. The length of the prison sentence stretching out in front of her now may have had a significant psychological effect on her. She spent much of her time in various convict prisons petitioning for release or quarrelling with staff and other inmates (she had fights and arguments with six prisoners on separate occasions for which she was punished by loss of remission, solitary confinement, and having to pay for the damage she did to prison property).

In 1883 she wrote to the Secretary of State stating that she has worked hard in prison and if liberated at this stage of her sentence her brother would look after her. Her petition was refused. Perhaps encouraged by the letters she received from her daughter Mary Ellen in St. Marys Industrial School, Eltham, she continued to petition for early release. In 1886 she made two requests to be released to the care of the Discharged Prisoners' Aid Society (DPAS), or to the Refuge.

In October that year she was released to the London DPAS in Charing Cross Road with nine months of her sentence left to serve. Re-united with her daughter after serving a good proportion of her life in prison, she never re-offended again.

72. Sarah Newbold (born 1862, Aston, Birmingham) Licence no. A46668/ 7615

Counterfeit George II spade guinea (*Authors' Collections*)

Coining was the production of counterfeit currency and uttering was the passing of false currency to another person (an offence normally committed by women). These offences, whilst still being seen as serious, were considered to be treasonous in the eighteenth century – and the death penalty was regularly applied to counterfeiters. Similarly, counterfeiters in the nineteenth century were severely punished, usually with long penal sentences. Counterfeit money undermined public confidence in currency, cheques, and promissory notes, and therefore undermined all of the processes of exchange that the burgeoning capitalist system relied upon.

Sarah grew up in a respectable Staffordshire household. Her father William Newbold was a 'hardworking man', working at Yates and Co, Toolmakers for nine years (in 1882) and he also held a previous well-paid position for ten years. Her brother-in-law Charles Evans was a 'thoroughly respectable' hairdresser at 101 Lancaster Street, Birmingham, married to Jane's sister Harriet (born c. 1851). Sister Emma Morton was married and lived in Derby.

However, Sarah seemed to have a turbulent teenage life. Between the ages of 16 and 20 she had been convicted of four felonies (stealing clothes mainly), disorderly prostitution, and had spent several months inside Birmingham Prison. In July 1881 she was convicted of 'uttering counterfeit coin' at Warwick Assize Court, and sentenced to six months' custody and twelve months' police supervision. Not learning her lesson, she was again convicted of 'uttering' soon after her release on 28 April 1882.

This time Stafford Assizes handed down a sentence of five years' penal servitude. In October she requested permission to apply to change her religion 'because I have always attended the Catholic church until I came into prison, and because my husband is a Catholic and my two children were christened as Catholics and I love the religion and would be more content as a Catholic'– the forms supplied, but she later changed her mind. Nevertheless, the prison governor wrote to Sarah's father regarding her religion – the reply states that she had been christened a protestant in St Clements Church, Nechells, and brought up a Protestant.

Although she was not visited by her family whilst in prison, they had not abandoned her, and her children were looked after by her sister. Sarah constantly asked about her children, and was clearly suffering in prison. In May 1882 she had attempted to hang herself in her cell. She also committed over thirty breaches of prison regulations whilst on her sentence, including fighting, swearing, threatening staff 'whilst in temper', and breaking prison property. She was punished by having to wear a canvas dress, suffering a penal diet of bread and water, solitary confinement, and loss of remission, which eventually resulted in her only being released on licence one month from the expiration of her five-year sentence.

On 5 April 1887 Sarah was released to her intended place of abode with her brother-in-law and sister. However, there was no trace of her at that address when the census was taken in 1891. Aged 29, there was no further trace of her in criminal or in census records. She had possibly married, maybe moved on, and hopefully she had reformed, living a full and honest life with her children.

73. Bridget O'Donnell (born c.1843, Ireland) Licence no. 70738/7535

Bridget O'Donnell (*The National Archives*)

Kirkdale Industrial School operated between 1843 and 1904. Originally it was a workhouse school but was later made into an Industrial School in the 1850s. These schools operated to care for and educate vagrant or neglected children and were the result of campaigns by social reformers such as Mary Carpenter. The Industrial Schools Act (1857) provided some regulation, but most were privately-run, initiated by parishes, charities or philanthropists. At first Kirkdale School held 400 children and though it expanded quickly, to 1150, it was still unable to accommodate all of the destitute children of Liverpool, many of whom remained in workhouses. Children were given a basic and religious education and taught trades and skills.

Bridget O'Donnell (or MacDonald/McDonald) had over fifty summary convictions for drunkenness, prostitution and fighting as well as two convictions for theft by her mid-20s. She lived in Liverpool, but had been born in Ireland. Her two previous convictions ensured a seven-year penal servitude sentence when she was convicted for stealing a watch in 1868. She was sent to Walton, where she had served many short sentences, to await her removal to Millbank. By July, she had completed separate confinement and she was moved to Woking. She spent the following four years in Woking and committed seven offences against prison rules.

Bridget was punished for quarrelling, bad language, fighting, breaking cell windows, and receiving items from other prisoners. She spent a total of thirty-two days in close confinement and she lost ninety-seven days remission. She was released on licence early but it could have been earlier. She left Woking in October 1873, thirty-four months early and headed back to Liverpool.

During her time in prison, she tried to write to family or friends, though letters were often returned. Her daughter, Mary Ann was in Kirkdale Industrial School. Back in Liverpool, she was still on licence and a conviction for being drunk and disorderly in August 1874 would cost her dearly. Her licence was revoked and she was returned to Millbank. After separation, she was sent to Woking, and discharged when her sentence expired in August 1876. Bridget continued to write to Mary Ann and received replies. She also continued to get in trouble, for singing, insolence, bad language, fighting and being abusive to staff; she lost class marks, remission marks and was placed in the penal ward for a month.

Bridget did not offend for the next few years but on Christmas Eve 1883 she was committed to Walton for larceny. On 7 January 1884 she received a five-year sentence. Now in her early forties, Bridget returned to Millbank. She was received at Woking in July 1884; she was excused from work due to weak lungs; had defective eye impeding her ability to read and write and she had a head injury due to a fall. Bridget wrote letters to women in the Scotland Road area of the city; one may have been her daughter, but all were returned as 'not known'. She continued to offend in prison, losing remission marks and spending more time in close confinement.

In February 1886 she was moved to Fulham. Five months later she obtained 'first class' status and despite a disturbance in the laundry was given a conditional licence to the East End Refuge. After nine months she was allowed to leave. Bridget does not seem to have committed any crimes for at least the next five years but unsurprisingly we lose track on her after her release.

74. Fanny Oliver (born 1841, Barwell, Worcestershire) Licence no. 2066/7402

Advert for arsenical soap
(*Authors' Collections*)

Arsenic has a long history as a fast-acting substance used by poisoners. It is assumed that many murderers in the mediaeval period used arsenic to despatch rivals; and famous poisoners of the nineteenth century include Florence Maybrick, who was convicted of soaking flypapers to obtain arsenic, then putting it into her husband's meals. From 1836, the Marsh Test could be used to detect the presence of arsenic in the victim's body, and from then on the detection of arsenic poisoning made it less popular amongst murderers. However, because arsenic was used in cosmetic products, cleaning products, and as a sexual aphrodisiac, it was still possible that arsenic could accidentally find its way into food, as Fanny asserted.

Fanny was born in Barwell, near Birmingham, in 1841; and only ever troubled the courts once in her life, in 1869, when she murdered her husband. She was sentenced to death by the court, but had the sentence commuted to life imprisonment. As soon as she entered convict prison she was marked down as a woman that suffered from hysteria. As the Medical Officer noted in November 1869, 'this woman has always been low and desponding, I have always had her closely watched'.

Fanny petitioned to have her sentence mitigated just after Christmas 1869 but the request was refused as there were no grounds to further reduce the severity of her sentence. In the next few years she made further requests to have her sentence reduced on the grounds that she was innocent. She also asked to have a likeness of her husband and a lock of her husband's hair placed in her cell. The Medical Officer deemed this unwise, and all of her requests were refused.

In 1874 she petitioned the Home Office to release her on the grounds that she was innocent, and this time she came up with a reason: the arsenic that had been found in her husband's body, the critical fact which had led to her conviction, could have got there accidentally since she used arsenic to clean the house. As her husband helped her to clean, some of the poison may have found its way into his body. Similarly, the prussic acid in his body was only there because he used it to alleviate headaches. The Home Office found no grounds to release her.

By 1876 she had made another three petitions, all fruitless. In the last one she explained that she had not been, as was alleged at her trial, having an affair with a man called Burgess. In fact, she said, she had only seen Burgess three times since she was a girl, although she had lent him £2 on the last occasion. Her attempts to involve the Earl of Dudley in petitioning for release on her behalf fell on stony ground, as did all other attempts to have her sentence mitigated. The Medical Officer believed that the long sentence was further exacerbating her fragile mental state, but that there were substantial medical grounds for release.

After being diagnosed with heart disease in 1883 she again petitioned for release, this time on medical grounds. The Home Office requested that the prison give her a medical examination every three months to monitor her health. However, all of Fanny's requests for clemency were refused until 1886 when she was released on licence to the care of her uncle. She had by this time served sixteen years of her life sentence. Fanny Oliver never offended again, and she died in Dudley in 1898 aged 57.

75. Mary Ann Pearson (born c.1842, Birmingham) Licence no. 10994

Roman mosaic, Ostia Antica, Rome
(*Authors' Collections*)

Mosaics date back to classical antiquity. Mary was one of a number of women convicts who were employed in Woking Invalid Convict Prison's mosaic workshop, which was created to give women convicts employment at light labour, and became very well known. Many of the mosaics in the crypt of St Paul's Cathedral were constructed from pieces of coloured marble broken up by female convicts at Woking. Similarly, one of the mosaic floors at the Victoria and Albert Museum is known as the 'opus criminale', as it originated from Woking Invalid Prison.

Mary Ann Pearson (aka Devanny) was born in Birmingham around 1842. She worked, as so many people did in Birmingham in the nineteenth century, in the 'toy' trade ('toy' being a word for any kind of small metal goods) – as a polisher. She first appears in the court records in July 1866, charged at Birmingham Police Court with stealing a pair of trousers in a public house. She received twenty-one days' hard labour. Later in the same year Mary appeared at Birmingham Sessions, accused of stealing a shawl, and was sentenced to twelve-months' imprisonment.

These two fairly minor brushes with the criminal justice system unfortunately do not appear to have deflected Mary from a life of crime. On 30 December 1867 she was found guilty of once more stealing a shawl (such goods were easily pawned and relatively expensive), and sentenced to seven years' penal servitude. She was transferred from Stafford Prison to Millbank Prison on 10 February 1868 and was allocated to light labour only, being found to suffer from numerous ailments including catarrh, tapeworm (a result of a poor diet and hygiene) and rheumatism. She was moved to Parkhurst Infirmary and then to Woking Invalid Prison.

Her illnesses appear to have suppressed her rebellious spirit for a couple of years, but on 27 June 1870 she was admonished for the first of over twenty offences that she would commit whilst in prison. She clearly had a problem with authority, being disciplined on numerous occasions for disobedience of orders and for quarrelling with other prisoners. Despite these offences, she was released on licence with two years and nine months of her sentence not served. She was first discharged to the Eagle House Refuge (for female Roman Catholic prisoners) and then released on conditional licence.

Mary seems to have kept out of trouble for a number of years, and continued with her trade as a polisher. However, in April 1880 she once more appeared in court on a charge of larceny, being found guilty of stealing a jacket and a pair of trousers in collusion with Jane Newbold (who also appears in this book). She was sentenced in Birmingham to a further seven years' penal servitude and once again entered Millbank before being transferred again to Woking where she carried out light labour in the mosaic shop. Despite her continued poor health, Mary carried on being a nuisance to the prison authorities, offending throughout her second stay in the prison.

She was released on licence for a second time, but once again was soon back before the courts, being found guilty of stealing 20 yards of oilcloth at Warwick Assizes on 23 February 1885. Her second licence was revoked and she was sentenced to twelve months' imprisonment and the remainder of her previous sentence. She was released on special licence on 24 February 1886 and subsequently disappears from all official records.

76. George Pobjoy (born c.1816, near Bath) Licence no. 405

Convicts returning to the hulks after work (*H. Mayhew and J. Binny*, The Criminal Prisons of London and Scenes of London Life, *1862*)

George spent over three months of his 1850 sentence of seven years' transportation in the *Stirling Castle* prison hulk. The ship was used as an invalid hulk, where convicts unable to carry out hard labour were confined. The system of hulks dated back to a 1789 Act of Parliament, which established that 'Where any Male Person shall be lawfully convicted of Grand Larceny, or any other Crime, except Petty Larceny, for which he shall be liable by Law to be transported to any Parts beyond the Seas, it shall and may be lawful for the Court to order and adjudge that such Person shall be punished by being kept on Board Ships or Vessels properly accommodated for the Security, Employment, and Health of the Persons to be confined therein...'

George Pobjoy (had his first brush with the law before he was aged 20, being accused in 1836 with a fellow quarry labourer of stealing jewellery from the house of his master, quarryman William Weare of Combe Down, Somerset. He was found 'not guilty' and does not appear in criminal records again until 1849, when he was found guilty at Somerset County Sessions of stealing a bundle of leather in Combe Down and sentenced to four months' imprisonment. On 21 October 1850 he was found guilty of the larceny of a bridle rein. As he had a previous conviction, George was sentenced to seven years' transportation.

George appears to have fallen ill whilst in Pentonville Prison and was transferred to the *Stirling Castle* Invalid Prison hulk on 17 December 1851. On 30 March 1852 he was sent back to serve the remainder of his sentence in Portsmouth Prison. After serving half of his sentence (all of it within England), his licence was granted on 14 February 1854 and he was released on 3 March 1854. However, on 1 August 1856 he was accused of the violent highway robbery of a medical man, Mr William Harding, at Combe Down. It was reported that George carried out the garrotting in partnership with Harriet Trueman (with whom he cohabited). It is highly likely that Harriet Trueman was also known as Harriet Vennell, by whom George had fathered two children, and who had previously been convicted in 1840 of stealing a shawl and coral necklace, being sentenced to three months' imprisonment. George and Harriet were caught red-handed; 'upon three officers going to the spot where the robbery took place, about 2 o'clock in the morning, they found the two prisoners searching the road with a lighted candle [looking for incriminating evidence] which they extinguished as soon as they saw the police approaching.' *(The Times*, 1 May 1856). Harriet was sentenced to eight years' penal servitude, whilst George received a sentence of ten years' penal servitude overseas. On 18 September 1857 he sailed aboard the *Nile* convict ship, bound for Western Australia. He arrived in Perth on 1 January 1858. On 28 February 1861, George received his ticket-of-leave, being recorded as a 'woodsman working on his own account'. He received a conditional pardon on 11 June 1864.

George stayed in the Perth area, being arrested several times for vagrancy and drunkenness, and in November 1884 was admitted to the Mount Eliza Invalid Depot, Perth. This was a charitable institution for down-and-outs, and George stayed there or in the associated Waterside Depot until 1893, when he was found drowned in the Swan River on 19 June, with an open verdict being recorded by the coroner.

77. Jane Potts (born c.1833, Manchester) Licence no. 70738/7535

Chorlton Union Workhouse
(*Authors' Collections*)

Chorlton Union Workhouse (sometimes referred to as Withington workhouse), was rebuilt in 1855. The old workhouse had held 300 inmates on Stretford New Road but had become inadequate as the surrounding population had grown. The new building opened on Nell Lane, Withington and the site also included a cemetery which served the workhouse and the district until 1920. The building held up to 1500 inmates and cost around £53,000. In the 1860s a pavilion plan hospital was added to the north of the workhouse. In 1915 a single new Manchester Union was formed and the workhouse was renamed Withington Hospital, later becoming part of the National Health Service.

Jane Coppock married Henry Potts in Chorlton, Lancashire in 1861; she was 28 years old. She was 36 when she was convicted of her first offence, stealing a pair of boots and she spent one month in Manchester prison. In December 1870 she was again convicted for stealing boots and received a three-month sentence. On her third conviction, also for stealing boots in January 1872, the court sentenced her to twelve months' imprisonment and seven years' police supervision.

Two years later Jane was committed to Manchester Prison on charges of larceny, stealing a shawl, and at the March Sessions she was convicted. She was sentenced to seven years' penal servitude and seven years' police supervision. She was sent from Manchester Prison to Millbank in mid-April. She regularly wrote to and received letters from Henry; and by this time they had had five children, four of whom were living and they resided in Hulme. She progressed well at school, her behaviour was good and after completing the separation stage of her sentence in December, she was moved to Fulham Prison. She continued to correspond with Henry and in 1877 she was informed that her brother had died. She asked the Governor about the possibility of going to the refuge and when she might be sent. In February 1878 her conditional licence was granted and she went to the Russell House Refuge, where she stayed for nine months until her release was permitted.

Just before Christmas 1881, Jane was arrested for stealing two-and-a-half pounds of beef; and was committed to Manchester Prison the next day, and her son, William visited her on Boxing Day. At the sessions she receives seven years' penal servitude. In March, she was sent to Millbank, where she wrote and received letters from her husband and William during the year. In August she was received at Woking Prison. She wanted to be excused from school, claiming she could read and write but the Chaplain would not approve, yet it was later approved by the Medical Officer. She continued to correspond with William, though at the end of 1883, one of her letters to Henry is sent back. It is not clear what happened but she does not receive any further letters from Henry (he may have died) though she regularly communicates with William.

In April 1885 she was admonished after being insolent to the Assistant Matron. She petitioned for the remission of the unexpired term of her previous sentence, but she was told she must serve another year of the remnant. In October 1886 she was released on special licence and returns to Hulme, to be received by her son.

By 1891 Jane was in Chorlton workhouse and for the next two decades she regularly admits herself to the workhouse for long periods; and she dies there in 1913.

78. Annie Price (born c.1840, Cork, Ireland) Licence no. A2291/7530

A female prisoner wearing a canvas dress (*H. Mayhew and J. Binny*, The Criminal Prisons of London and Scenes of London Life, *1862*)

The canvas dress was used for the punishment of female prisoners. The dress had straps with restricted the movement of the arms and body of the person wearing it but it was not as restrictive as a strait jacket which was used for most difficult and recalcitrant prisoners. Prisoners were placed in canvas dresses for periods usually for 24 hours and this might also be accompanied by the use of hobbles. Hobbles or fetters were like handcuffs but for the legs, they restricted movement of the legs but did not prevent it entirely. Some prisoners were placed in a canvas dress during time in their cell (when not at work) for up to three months at a time, though it could be removed early if they behaved.

Annie Price had a number of aliases (Lane, McGuire, O'Brien, O'Brian) and spent a considerable proportion of her life in the prisons of England. She served three sentences of penal servitude during her life, the first of which she served the whole term of four years' penal servitude after being convicted of robbery and personal violence by Newcastle-upon-Tyne Sessions in November 1863. She was sent to Millbank and then six months later to Parkhurst, where she committed thirty-two prison offences. For these offences she was regularly being placed in close confinement, on a bread and water diet; and often in a canvas dress for 24 hours and in 'hobbles' (leg ties, restricting movement). She was discharged in November 1867 having lost all of her remission.

In 1869 she spent six months in Birmingham Prison for stealing a purse and money; and just under a year later she was committed to Leeds Prison for fifteen months for stealing money from the person. Shortly after her release from Leeds Prison she had been living as the wife of Charles Robinson who she stabbed to death on 23 October 1871. She received a twelve-year sentence of penal servitude for manslaughter and was sent again to Millbank in January 1872. Nine days after her arrival she was placed on a penal diet for twenty-eight days; and to wear a canvas dress for three months without report, as well as losing 112 remission marks; and to make up 540 stage marks for standing on her table, shouting, destroying thirty-six panes of glass, three blankets, two sheets, a rug, cell furniture and clothes.

Annie also requested to change from Protestant to Roman Catholic religion. She stated that she was a Roman Catholic and had been born one in Cork but had been told that Protestants got more privileges when in prison, which was not the case, and now she regretted stating this falsehood. Her change of religion was approved. She committed another five offences before she was moved to public works at Woking. She had been cautioned about her future conduct at Woking but she continued to commit various offences against the prison rules. She committed another forty-nine offences before she was released on licence to the Mission to Women, Wandsworth, two years and seven months early.

Five months later, Annie was in Chester Prison on charges of larceny. She was accused of stealing money from the person of Ellen Henderson at Birkenhead. Once again she was sent to Millbank and then on to Fulham Prison where she worked in the garden. She committed a further ten prison offences and was released twenty-one days early to Cheshire DPAS in Birkenhead where she reported herself the next day. After her sentence expired she moved to Warrington; whilst we have lost track of her, she does not appear to have committed any further crimes.

79. **Joseph Quarmby** (born 1822, Huddersfield) Licence no. A38690/ 45414

Prisoners were required to work in prison, and one form of hard labour was to pick between two and six lbs of oakum per day. Hempen rope was covered in tar in order to caulk (or fill in) the gaps between planks on ships. In order to re-use oakum, prisoners were required to disentangle the strands of the fibrous hemp or rope. Because the tar had hardened the fibres, this was an extremely unpleasant task that cut away at the skin, and caused considerable soreness to the hands of the picker. Other forms of hard labour included quarrying, building naval fortifications, sawing, tailoring, shoemaking, laundry work (especially for women), sowing mail sacks, and working in the kitchen, or prison farm.

Prisoners picking oakum
(*H. Mayhew and J. Binny*, The Criminal Prisons of London and Scenes of London Life, *1862*)

Joseph was convicted for larceny under a number of aliases around West Yorkshire. Coming from a family of stonemasons, he was tried for stealing mason's tools three times between 1853 and 1860, and he spent a number of months in Yorkshire prisons. In 1868, aged 44, Joseph had a bad fall and injured his back; and his later prison records indicate that he had a severe chronic rupture, along with being deaf, weak lungs, being scarred and having possibly being of unsound mind. After stealing more tools in the 1860s, he was finally given penal servitude (seven years) at Salford Sessions in 1870. In prison he was first given stonemasonry to complete, but refused to work at this, or many other labour tasks. During his sentence he was punished for insolence, refusing to pick sufficient amounts of oakum (on countless occasions), and for complaining about warders, for example: 'I wish to complain that Assistant Warder A.R. Pearce ill-used me yesterday, knocking my teeth out and kicking him so as to make his rupture come down.' He was punished for bringing a false charge against the officer, and his future complaints about warder Pearce also fell on deaf ears. On Christmas Eve 1875 he asked to be placed in a new cell as he was anxious to turn over a new leaf. He then committed twelve new breaches of prison rules in 1876, before being released from Portland.

In 1878 he stole more tools and his sentence this time was ten years' penal servitude and five years' police supervision. Again he complained about brutality. The Medical Officer stated that Joseph was 'of weak mind complained that he had been kicked in the testicles by a warder. On examination I find that there is a large bruise on his scrotum evidently caused by a rather violent blow, nor can this injury have been self-inflicted.' The matter was investigated and the warder concerned stated that Joseph 'refused to take [his] clothes off and attempted to strike him with his urinal, and that he was obliged to use his staff but did not kick him'.

Further refusals to do as he was told earned Joseph many punishments over the next few years, and he seems to have been deemed to breach prison rules much more than the average prisoner. On three more occasions, in different prisons, he alleged more assaults by staff, each of which was dismissed as self-inflicted.

He was released on licence in 1887, with a year unexpired on his license. He was, however, re-convicted in 1888 and gaoled for six months. The newspaper reported that he had escaped penal servitude because it was a small theft; and because he wanted to go back to convict prison as he was ill and got better treatment in prison than outside it. After a couple more thefts from the workhouse where he was housed, he died in Huddersfield, aged 82.

80. William Quickfall (born 1803, North Caldy, Lincolnshire) Licence no. 92317/22454

Crowle village centre (*Authors' Collections*)

Constable Waddingham was a member of the Lindsey Division of Lincolnshire County Constabulary, which had been founded in 1857. Crowle was a small village, but with five public houses, the police must have had their hands full at times. A village police station and lockup for Crowle was approved in 1865; the building provided accommodation for a sergeant and a constable, together with a single cell and an exercise yard. Surviving police records show that Acting Sergeant Summers was immediately dismissed for cowardice as a result of Quickfall's shooting of PC Waddingham in 1866.

William Quickfall appears to have led something of a charmed life with regard to his contact with the criminal justice system. He makes his first recorded appearance in court records in February 1850, when he was found guilty of trespassing in pursuit of game and sentenced to two months' imprisonment at Crowle, Lincolnshire.

For the next sixteen years he continued to live at Crowle without incident with his wife and nephew. However, on the morning of 10 June 1866 he was spotted on the estate of a landed gentleman, emerging from a wood and carrying a gun. Two police officers, Constable John Waddingham and Acting Sergeant Summers gave chase, and despite being 63 years of age, Quickfall was not caught up with for some three-quarters of a mile, until he was confronted by a dyke. Turning to the officers, he 'reputedly threatened to fire rather than be taken'. Waddingham ignored this threat and got to within three yards of Quickfall, who then fired one barrel of the shotgun. Waddingham was hit below the left shoulder, causing major damage to his arm (which was eventually amputated). Quickfall then made good his escape, and a reward of £50 was subsequently offered for his capture. Quickfall survived on the moors for several days, before making for his brother-in-law's house, where his relative reported him to the police and claimed the reward.

Quickfall was tried at Lincoln Assizes on 24 July 1866 for attempted murder, but was found guilty of wounding with intent to cause grievous bodily harm and sentenced to five years' penal servitude. He was released early on licence from Dartmoor Prison in July 1870 and returned to his family at Crowle. His behaviour and temper did not however improve.

In November 1881 he was sentenced to four months for unlawful assault, and in January 1884 history almost repeated itself, as Quickfall was charged with discharging a gun at a solicitor, James Elmhirst, after being caught poaching on Mr Elmhirst's land. Quickfall stated that there was no powder in his gun and that he had only fired in order to frighten Mr Elmhirst. He was once again committed to trial at Lincoln Assizes, but was only charged with night poaching and assault, receiving a sentence of twelve months' imprisonment.

In January 1886 at the age of 83 he was once more brought before the court, this time charged by Superintendent Taylor with night poaching and threatening to shoot a police officer. Quickfall had been caught red-handed and stated 'I have shot one man before and will kill you'. The officer let him escape but he was soon recaptured. However, several witnesses (including his brother) swore an alibi for Quickfall and he was rather surprisingly given the benefit of the doubt and discharged. A William Quickfall, aged 88, died in the winter of 1890 at Thorne in the West Riding; and it is probable that this was the end of a 'notorious poacher' and somewhat lucky individual.

81. **George Renyard** (born 1841, Beaulieu, Hants.) Licence no. 78350/22559

Catching a poacher (The Graphic *newspaper*, *1875*)

Setting traps for a few rabbits, or taking some fish from the local landowner's pond, was a popular countryside pursuit in the eighteenth and nineteenth centuries. It provided a necessary supplement to meagre diets for the labouring poor in the countryside. The practice was condoned within agricultural communities, although landowners pressed for heavy penalties, and often employed armed private gamekeepers to protect their game. In some areas poaching gangs raided the countryside taking large numbers of animals or fish, and pitched battles between police and poachers, sometimes resulted in serious violence, even deaths.

George Renyard grew up in the New Forest with his family, finding work in his teens as an agricultural labourer in the 1850s. Although he was convicted in 1859 of the dangerous-sounding offence of 'firing a gun within 50 feet of a highway', this was really a poaching offence rather than a wild shooting. Accordingly, he, and his two co-defendants, were sentenced only to a fine. He was first sent to prison in 1863, for drunkenness. The newspaper that reported his twenty-one-day sentence described him as 'an old offender', despite George only having come before the courts on two occasions. Possibly he was well known as a poacher by this time, and despite only having been caught once, he may have had a reputation for taking game on a regular basis.

It was probably a well-deserved reputation, for on 2 March 1865 George was convicted of being a member of a poaching gang, and whilst out with the gang he wounded a constable who was trying to arrest him for poaching. The police officer survived, but the offence was a serious one, and he was sentenced to seven years' penal servitude. He was first imprisoned in Pentonville Convict Prison before being transferred to Portsmouth. However, once the authorities there discovered that he had a cousin already in that prison, was well-acquainted with the Portsmouth area, and had many friends in the region, he was quickly moved to another convict prison – Portland.

He was a fairly well-behaved prisoner, and did not overly trouble the prison authorities. He was released with nearly two years of his sentence left to serve, and he fulfilled his licence conditions without breach. Indeed, he made a virtue of his good behaviour in prison and on licence when he was brought back to the courts for trespassing on land and taking fruit illegally. He protested that he was out collecting winter berries when two other men joined him in the same pursuit. Although convicted, he was only fined, when the sentence could have been much more severe.

George remained outside of prison, and seemingly remained in a happy marriage, his wife bearing him a son in 1875. His son grew up to be a gardener, whilst George carried on working as an agricultural labourer in the same village he grew up in, Boldre (Hampshire), until he died in 1906, aged 72.

After his 'berrying' escapade the only time he had been in court was on 19 November 1884 when he was accused of allowing his donkey to illegally graze in New Forest meadowland (Verderers' Court, Lyndhurst). His six-shilling fine was a far cry from the seven years of penal servitude he had experienced some twenty years previously.

82. Alfred Rhodes (born Brighouse, Yorkshire, 1853) Licence no. A46420/ 45236

Borstal Schoolroom c.1906 (*Public Domain*)

The term 'Borstal' became synonymous with young offenders as a result of the former Rochester Prison being converted in 1902 to an experimental juvenile prison for male offenders between the ages of 16 and 21. The system was extended to the rest of the country in 1908, dealing with both male and female offenders. The separation of juveniles from adults was introduced as 'ordinary detention in prison [...] cannot, even with the greatest care and the best possible arrangements, allow of that specialization and individual attention which is essential, if a real impression is to be made on the younger prisoners' (*Report of the Commissioner of Prisons*, 1908).

Alfred Rhodes' offending pattern follows a fairly typical trajectory: troublesome as a young man following the death of his father whilst he was still a young boy; brushes with the law for drink-related offences; a more serious charge of larceny followed by one major felony, resulting in a long prison sentence; marriage; children and a stable family life leading to desistance. He was baptised in Brighouse, Yorkshire on 5 June 1853. His father John was a coalminer who died whilst Alfred was in his early years. Alfred lived with his six siblings and widowed mother throughout his teenage years, following in the family tradition and becoming a coal hewer. His first recorded brush with the law came in November 1874 when he was found guilty of being drunk and disorderly and sentenced to fourteen days' imprisonment.

Four further drink-related offences were recorded against Alfred's character between 1874 and 1880, each resulting in short terms of imprisonment. However, on 29 November 1880 he was brought before the magistrates at Bradford Sessions and found guilty of the larceny from the person of a gold sovereign. He was sentenced to twelve months' imprisonment. Two further minor infringements of the law (being drunk and disorderly and using obscene language) followed in the next two years, and by this time he had earned the reputation of being 'of known bad character'. On 2 April 1883 he was found guilty at Wakefield Sessions of being found in possession of housebreaking tools, after a previous conviction for felony (his stealing of the sovereign in 1880). He was caught red-handed by the police along with George Clegg, another individual with a poor record, in possession of skeleton keys and jemmies.

As a consequence, he was sentenced to a period of five years' penal servitude to be followed by three years' police supervision. Throughout the term of his imprisonment, he maintained regular contact with his widowed mother Mary. A letter to his mother dated 11 January 1886 was suppressed by the prison authorities as in it he claimed that he was innocent of the crime – '... there on case to be a shamed of me becase I don no crime', and he also stated that in prison you '... have to learn to be as false as a monky'. He spent over three years at Borstal Prison (also known as Rochester Prison), before being released on licence on 23 March 1887, with thirteen months of his sentence unserved. On 30 December 1889 he married a weaver, Mary Ineson, at Batley, Yorkshire, and they subsequently produced two children: Brice (born 1893) and Sarah (born 1895). Alfred's widowed mother moved in with them and Alfred regained employment as a coal hewer and miner.

In the 1911 census he is recorded as a 'coal hewer' (miner) living at Ardsley, Yorkshire with his wife and teenage son and daughter.

83. Mary Ann Roberts (born 1852, Liverpool) Licence no. 7413

Female staff in female prisons had been legally required since 1823, when Elizabeth Fry's (see image) reforms for female prisoners had been incorporated into the Gaols Act; female prisoners to be attended only by female officers. In the convict system, each wing had a matron and a number of assistant matrons, they usually lived in the prison. They worked long hours, 12, sometimes 15 hours per day and were subject to many rules and regulations on their lives. As in local prisons, matrons were supposed to be examples of ideal womanhood, demonstrating feminine virtues as role models for the inmates to adopt. In reality, most had social backgrounds similar to their charges.

Elizabeth Fry (*Public Domain*)

Mary Ann Roberts was from Liverpool and in 1879 she was convicted of wounding a police constable, James Kavanagh, with the intent to commit grievous bodily harm. She received a sentence of ten years' penal servitude. Mary had forty-six previous convictions between 1852, when she was about 14 years old, and November 1878. In examining the case, the stipendiary magistrate, Mr Raffles, had considered Kavanagh to be so dangerously ill that he visited him to take a deposition. Mary was single, had no occupation, she could read and her health was fair, but she suffered from a fractured skull and 'depression in the occipital [base of the skull]'; and when she entered the prison she had syphilitic ulcers on both legs.

Mary's bad behaviour continued in prison as she was frequently in trouble, breaking the rules and was violent to prisoners and staff. After entry to Millbank Prison and a quarrel with prisoner Mary Hamilton, where she struck her in the face, she was placed under medical observation. They noted she was 'very excitable and there cannot be a doubt that the extensive injury to her skull and brain makes her at times unreasonable'. She was transferred to Woking and continued to get into trouble. Mary threatened prisoner D136 Johnson and was placed in a penal cell for 24 hours, but the next day repeated the threats to Johnson and to Assistant Matron Hadden. She was placed in the penal cell for twenty-eight days. But her violent and disruptive behaviour continued and in the following four years she assaulted a number of prisoners and staff as well as frequently causing a disturbance through breaking cell windows and furniture, throwing clothes, using abusive language, screaming and singing. She assaulted other prisoners on at least ten occasions; she assaulted B32 Cook a few times, striking her a severe blow cutting her eye and pulling her hair; and later she attacked her with a stone; she fought with other inmates in the airing yard, she bit them; and she was found in possession of a piece of steel to be used as a knife. During one period she was being punished for incidents about once a month, she also spent time in the infirmary for debility and for ulceration of the cartilage in her knee.

When it came to release, Mary said that she did not have anyone who could receive her but wanted to go to a workhouse or a hospital. The Governor did not know a hospital that would take her but he did try as the Royal Free Hospital they wrote to say there were no beds. She was released to the East End Refuge in March 1886, though she must have behaved there or she would have been sent back. Later she returned to Liverpool.

In 1891 she was living with her brother in Barton-upon-Irwell. Mary Ann died five years later, when she was about 44 years old.

84. **Archibald Ross** (born c.1857, Stoer, Scotland) Licence no. A5152

Inverness Castle c.1715 (*Public Domain*)

Archibald Ross's first experience of prison life was spent in the North Block of Inverness Castle. It functioned as a small mixed-sex local gaol until 1902, when a new and much larger prison was constructed in an outlying rural parish of Inverness at Porterfield. It was recorded that, at the time of changeover from the original prison to the new HMP Inverness, 25 male and 10 female prisoners were transferred from the old gaol. The North Block then served for many years as the Inverness Sheriff Court. However, plans are currently being discussed to move the Sheriff's Court and open up the building as a tourist attraction in order to ensure its preservation.

Archibald Ross's background does not appear to be that of the average Victorian convict (i.e. working-class, poverty-stricken and ill-educated). He was born the son of John and Christina Ross. His father was a Free Church of Scotland minister and Archibald received an education commensurate with his father's position in society; in the 1871 census he is listed as a boarder at a boarding school in Scouriemore, Lairg.

In 1879 Archibald makes his first recorded appearance in court, when he was charged with theft at Edinburgh and received a sentence of ten days' imprisonment. Less than a week after being released from prison, he appeared at Glasgow court, again charged with theft, and was sentenced to twenty days' imprisonment. On 8 September 1880, the *Aberdeen Weekly Journal* reported on a case involving Archibald, in which he was found guilty of having 'on the morning of the 21st May, broken into Drummond Park, Inverness, the residence of Mr Donald Davidson, solicitor, and stolen a great variety of objects, chiefly silver plate'. Archibald was found guilty of theft after a previous conviction and sentenced to eight years' penal servitude.

On 5 October 1880 he was transferred to Pentonville Prison. He offended there almost immediately, being charged on 29 October with having his cell and utensils in a dirty condition. He lost remission marks and was put on a punishment diet for a day. Archibald continued to offend intermittently throughout his stay at Pentonville and was transferred to Chatham on 7 June 1881. He petitioned the Home Secretary on several occasions during his confinement and appears to have played on possible family connections through his father, with whom in kept in touch throughout his sentence. The Marquis of Stafford intervened on his behalf, as a letter from the Marquis requesting permission for an interview with Ross was received by the governor of Chatham on 11 November 1882, and on 21 November 1884 he received a prison visit from the Marquis in person. The Marquis (Cromartie Sutherland-Leveson-Gower KG) was also the 4th Duke of Sutherland, and was one of the largest landowners in Great Britain, owning over one-and-a-half-million acres in the Scottish Highlands.

Ross appears to have maintained his contact with the Duke of Sutherland, writing to him on two further occasions and also receiving correspondence with him. It is unclear as to the extent of the Duke's involvement with the family and Ross's particular circumstances; whilst Ross was released early on licence on 3 March 1887, with eighteen months' unserved, this period of licence was not unusual. Post-release, Archibald Ross largely disappears from the public record.

85. **Alice Ann Rowlands** (born 1859, Liverpool) Licence no. A45114/ 7538

> *There are now three refuges for female convicts, the Carlisle Memorial Refuge at Winchester; the Eagle House Refuge at Hammersmith, for Roman Catholics; and the Westminster Memorial Refuge, lately established at Streatham. One-hundred and seventeen women women passed through these refuges in 1871 out of a total of two-hundred and seventy-five who were discharged from sentences of penal servitude.*

(*Extract of Report from International Penitentiary Congress of London, 1872*)

Alice Ann Rowlands was born and lived in Liverpool, she fell into crime as a teenager and at the age of 13 was sentenced to five years in a juvenile reformatory, preceded by ten days in prison. However, less than a month after her release she was back in prison, remanded for riotous behaviour but then later discharged. In the next few years she continued to commit minor offences and served short sentences for workhouse offences, drunkenness and stealing clothing, all crimes suggesting poverty. In December 1882 she was convicted of housebreaking and sentenced to twelve months' imprisonment. Her previous convictions ensured that in February 1884 when she was found guilty of larceny (stealing a shirt and singlet from one James Pearson) she was sentenced to five years' penal servitude.

Russell House Refuge as it was later known, opened in 1872 as the Westminster Memorial Refuge of the Royal Society for the Assistance of Discharged Prisoners for Protestant Women, and was based at 32 Charing Cross, Streatham, London. During the 1870s and 1880s it was heavily used by the convict system for women prisoners who were released to this refuge for a period on conditional licence (usually between six and nine months) before being fully licensed to their home. The refuge was active in helping women to emigrate to the United States. In 1888, the refuge was taken over by a congregation of Roman Catholic sisters and became a refuge for reformed prostitutes rather than prisoners.

Alice spent the initial weeks of her sentence at Walton Prison before she was sent to Millbank. She wrote and received letters from her father and aunt, all of whom lived in the Toxteth Park area of Liverpool. She worked sewing in her cell but appears to have behaved well. After six months at

Millbank, she was moved to Woking and put to work in the laundry. At Woking, Alice got into trouble on five occasions. Her first offence was for provoking and fighting with a prisoner called Jackson on their way back from the chapel, she was sent to close confinement for one day and she lost twelve remission marks. A couple of months later, she lost twelve remission marks for quarrelling with prisoner Williams, whilst in the infirmary. Alice received regular treatment for gynaecological problems and had a non-malignant breast tumour removed.

Alice was again in trouble, nine months later, she was placed in close confinement for three days and lost twelve remission marks for fighting with prisoner Hand and for singing in the hall. She received another day's punishment in close confinement for being very rude to the Assistant Superintendent, who had prevented her from leaving the mosaic tile room in which she was working. Two months later, she was found with her light on for cooking in her cell and with two pieces of steel hidden in her petticoat. She was demoted from second class to probation, sent to close confinement for three days and she lost twenty-four remission marks.

Just over five months later, she was released on conditional licence, having served two years and three months. Conditional licence ensured she was sent to the Russell House Refuge and in July 1887 she was permitted to leave there. Alice returned to Liverpool, married a shipyard labourer, Thomas Dowler and had a family. Despite her numerous offences in her youth and early twenties, Alice did not commit any more crimes during her lifetime.

86. Esther Sanston (born c.1835, Bristol) Licence no. 54388/7551

WHOSE CHILDREN? – kind attention of the Benevolent is called to an APPEAL for AID [...] for the CHILDREN'S HOME in the shape of DONATIONS and SUBSCRIPTIONS, however small, will be thankfully received by Lady Crofton or Miss Pumfrey, at Battery House, Winchester, and by the Reverend A. G. Garland, 21 Southgate Street, Winchester

(*Advertisement in the* Hampshire Advertiser, *19 December 1874*)

Esther Sanston was known by numerous aliases during her life: Elizabeth Smith, Eliza Smith, Eliza Sanston, Eliza Mack and Eliza McEvoy, and often appeared in court under one of these assumed names. Fortunately however, her offending record together with her life whilst in prison are well documented. It appears that Esther was married and widowed by the age of 38, though neither the name of her first husband nor her maiden name is not known. She first appears in court records under the name of Elizabeth Smith, when she was found guilty of stealing

Battery House Refuge in Winchester was one of a handful of refuges created for female convicts. The government funded 50% of the costs, with the refuges expected to find the other 50% through charitable donations. Female convicts of good behaviour were released on conditional licence 9 months before their eventual release. Over ¾ of all female convicts entered such refuges, where they were allowed to associate freely in an effort to assimilate them back into public life. There was also a major problem with what to do with the children of parents who were both serving terms of penal servitude. In 1874, Sir Walter Crofton (former Director of Irish prisons) and his wife created a children's home in the Battery House Refuge in Winchester. Each child was estimated to cost £12 per year to home and the appeal in the *Hampshire Advertiser* (above) hoped to meet these costs.

a watch at Manchester City Sessions. She was sentenced to six months' imprisonment in November 1863. Three months after her release she was once more before the same court, charged with stealing a pocket-book and she received another six months' imprisonment.

Five years later, she was found guilty of stealing money as Elizabeth Mack at Manchester and sentenced to one month's imprisonment. In October 1869 she received another eighteen months at Manchester City Sessions in the name of Elizabeth Smith, for stealing a watch. In May 1872 she appeared at Salford Sessions, charged with stealing over £40 (then a considerable amount) from the person of Jabez Parker. She was sentenced in the name of Eliza McEvoy to seven years' penal servitude to be followed by seven years' police supervision.

She served her time at both Millbank and Woking prisons, and kept in regular contact with her married sister, Hannah Bradley. On 21 April 1876 she was removed on conditional licence to Battery House Refuge in Winchester. After staying there without incident for nine months she was released back into the community, and appears to have subsequently married a William Sans[t]on (possibly in 1878). However, this did not prevent her from re-offending in February 1879, when she was sentenced to ten years' penal servitude and seven years' police supervision for stealing two half-crowns 'from the person'. She appears to have spent much of her time in the infirmary at Woking, being diagnosed with both pneumonia and debility. Despite her recent marriage, she does not appear to have received any letters from her husband. On 16 March 1886 she petitioned the Secretary of State, praying for remission of her sentence and saying that she had friends who were willing to help her upon her release. She received a reply on 31 March stating that she would be considered for release when she had served a year of her remnant (the sentence remaining from her original breach of licence).

She was finally released on her second licence on 17 November 1886 and is last recorded in the 1891 census as living as a married hawker (her husband is not present) with her sister and brother-in-law in Beswick.

87. Peter Simpson (born c.1854, Melton Mowbray, Leicestershire) Licence no. 46469

Interior of a cheap lodging house, 1862
(*H. Mayhew and J. Binny*, The Criminal Prisons of London and Scenes of London Life, *1862*)

Cheap lodging houses were often the only kind of refuge that released convicts could afford. Conditions were often abysmal; many people could not even afford to pay for any type of bed, so instead would pay for 'a night on the line'. This entailed draping one's arms over a rope or line strung between two walls and attempting to sleep whilst draped over the line. Rollestone House in Leicester, where Simpson was lodging in 1911, remained in use as a cheap lodging house until the 1960s, with a painted sign on the wall stating '100 beds for men'.

Peter Simpson appears to have led a troubled and often violent life. On 28 May 1877 he was court-martialled for insubordination and desertion from the 1st Battalion of the 19th Regiment (The Green Howards). He was committed to the Ipswich County Gaol on 12 June. A little under six months later, he violently attacked a prison warder, Frederick Southgate, whilst he was being led down to the prison's exercise yard. He hit Southgate on the head several times, causing a great deal of bleeding and concussion, and was only prevented from continuing the murderous attack after being restrained by other prisoners.

At his trial, held at Chesterton Assizes (Cambridge) on 11 January 1878 it was revealed that the reason behind the attack lay in persistent allegations by the prisoner that Warder Southgate had been poisoning his food; he was heard to say at the time of the attack that 'I will kill you for tampering with my gruel and putting starch and laudanum in it.' He showed no remorse immediately after the attack; it was reported that upon another warder stating 'What a villain you must be to commit such a dastardly attack', Simpson replied 'I consider I should have only done my duty if I had killed the ******'. For the attack, Simpson was found guilty of attempted murder and received a sentence of ten years' penal servitude.

His prison folder clearly shows that his temper or mental state did not improve during this period of incarceration. After a brief stint at Pentonville he was transferred to Millbank, where it was reported that between April and August 1878 he was in the infirmary with 'deliriums' – he 'talks and bangs himself in his cell. Fancies his food tampered with. Inclined to be quarrelsome and fight with other prisoners. Clean in his habits. Will work well if allowed to do so'. It is clear that the prison authorities decided that he was not insane, but instead was feigning his symptoms. In his medical report dated 10 February 1882, a Dr Benshfield stated 'Peter Simpson is reported to use disgusting, abusive and threatening language from time to time, with occasional displays of violence [...]. In robust bodily condition and has increased 5lbs in weight since his reception at Woking', but after being assessed by a specialist, Simpson was described as his 'mental and physical health [being] good'. The report goes on to state that 'this convict has been pronounced by Dr Drushfield, the medical superintendent of Dunwood Asylum to be a malingerer'.

Despite having over two dozen offences against his prison record, Simpson was released on licence with ten months of his sentence unserved. He did not trouble the authorities again, but in the 1891 census he is listed as a tramp living in Nantwich Workhouse. He last appears in the records in the 1911 census, where he is recorded as a bricklayer's labourer, lodging at Rollestone House, Leicester (a cheap lodging house for men).

88. Bridget Smith (born c.1831, Ireland) Licence no. 3867

Armley Gaol (*Authors' Collections*)

Leeds Borough Gaol, located in the Armley district of the city, was opened in 1847. As one of the local prisons for the West Riding of Yorkshire, it held prisoners from the local courts and when it first opened there were 291 cells. Executions were also carried out there and the last execution took place there in 1961, a few years before the death penalty was suspended. The prison had been designed on a radial design with four wings stretching out from a central hub, a prominent design typical of mid-Victorian prison architecture. HMP Leeds is still in use today and remains a local prison serving the courts, it currently holds over 1200 male offenders and it is designated as a Category B prison.

Bridget Smith was found guilty of setting fire to a stack of barley in December 1866. The barley, the property of a farmer, Mr Bramley and had been seen alight by two officers from the West Ridging Constabulary, Superintendent Wardell and PC Smith, who had been travelling between Tadcaster and Leeds. Bridget had been seen coming from the stack and there were no other people visible in the field. When charged with destroying the two stacks, her only reply was that there had only been one. She was sentenced to five years' penal servitude.

Bridget had been born in Ireland, but little is known of her family, she was single and under next of kin had 'no friends'. She was Roman Catholic, she could not read or write and had been working as a field labourer. She was initially sent to Leeds Prison and then transferred to Millbank in January 1867; and then onto Parkhurst a week later.

After arrival she spent a couple of weeks in the infirmary with an ulcer. She committed a number of prison offences, she was admonished a few times for being rude, she spent time in close confinement for fighting and she lost fifty-six remission marks. A short time later she was confined to her cell and a week later was placed in close confinement for ten days and lost 224 remission marks for refusing to go to chapel and destroying the furniture in her cell. She carried on in a similar vein for some time and the Chief Medical Officer said that she was strange in her manner and seemed to indicate imbecility but he later stated that she need not be treated differently but that she was of 'little mental development'. In November 1868 she was placed in a padded cell for medical observation after she had attempted to strike the Matron with her cell broom, thrown her pitcher at her and used abusive and threatening language.

Bridget was later removed from medical observation with no further comment. In January 1869 her misbehaviour continued as she refused to go to chapel, destroyed prison property and she was rude to her officer when they refused to give her a new jacket. In February she was placed in handcuffs in her cell after destroying prison furniture, using abusive language and attempting to strike and threatening to kill the officer. She was also placed back on to first stage penal class and forfeited 360 remission marks. Five days later she was back in handcuffs and hobbles and on a bread and water diet after another incident in which she tore a quantity of hair from an officer's head. In April 1869 she was transferred to Woking; after threatening another officer she was again assessed by a medical officer but a month later was transferred to Millbank and released on licence to Eagle House Refuge in July 1871. She died in 1881.

89. Mary Smith (born c.1845, Dublin) Licence no. 7435

Woking Invalid Convict Prison
(*Authors' Collections*)

Many of the individuals who served time as convicts did not enjoy long periods of good health. Their diet was often bad, leading to stomach problems, and such a poor diet often left them especially vulnerable to common ailments such as bronchitis. Sexually transmitted diseases were also rife, as there was at the time no reliable or safe cure for syphilis or gonorrhoea. Mary appears to have been particularly unfortunate, suffering from a range of medical problems, including phthisis (consumption), menorrhagia (painful and heavy menstrual flows), lumbago, and bronchitis. Woking was constructed as a male invalid convict prison in 1858 and a female invalid convict prison followed on the neighbouring site in 1867.

Mary Smith was a prolific petty offender, with at least twenty-four convictions in various names including Mary Jackson and Bridget Robinson. She seems to have led a drunken and unstable life before being sentenced to seven years' penal servitude at Wakefield Sessions for stealing money from the person. Her recorded distinguishing marks testify to a hard life; she had two cuts to her left arm below the elbow, scars on her right arm, face and lips and had lost several teeth. She spent time in Millbank Prison before being transferred to Parkhurst, where she was often recorded as being in the prison infirmary with various mental illnesses ranging from 'debility' to 'the blues' (surprisingly this term dates from at least 1827 when used to describe depression). She was then transferred to the newly opened Woking Invalid Prison, from where she was released on licence to Eagle House Refuge in 1872. This was a state-run halfway house for Catholic women serving the last few months of their imprisonment, situated in Hammersmith, London and opened in 1866. Mary spent six months there before being released on licence in November 1872.

However, Mary was recommitted to Millbank in August 1873 for an unknown offence, and was transferred once more to Working Invalid Prison before being released in June 1876. Two months later she appeared at Barnsley Magistrates Court charged with highway robbery (stealing 8d from the person of George Berry). A contemporary newspaper report stated that 'it was shown that the female prisoner had been seventeen times in Leeds Gaol, and seven times in the Wakefield House of Correction'. She was committed for trial at Sheffield Sessions and sentenced to ten years' penal servitude and five years' police supervision. She spent the majority of this sentence in Woking, suffering from a range of both mental and physical illnesses including recurrent bouts of syphilis (it was not until the discovery of penicillin that the disease could be fully cured). Despite her obvious infirmity, she proved to be an unruly patient, often being admonished for various breaches of conduct, including attacking another prisoner.

Despite this, she was released early on licence on 7 August 1883, stating that she was going to Leeds. Just over a year later, she failed to report to Leeds police station (this would have been a condition of her five years' police supervision) and her licence was revoked. She was therefore returned to prison to serve out the remainder of her sentence. She was released on another licence four months before her sentence was due to expire, this time stating that she was going to stay with her sister Ellen Fox in Brewery Street, Leeds.

Mary disappears from the records after this date – whether or not she stopped her offending before her death remains unknown – perhaps her physical and mental state precluded her from carrying out any more offences.

90. Sarah Jane Smith (born 1839, Bradford) Licence no. 84143/7536

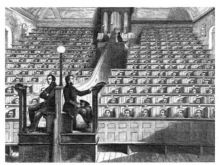

Separate system at Pentonville (*H. Mayhew and J. Binny,* The Criminal Prisons of London and Scenes of London Life, *1862*)

The Separate system originated in Philadelphia in 1829, and was gradually adopted as a way of curtailing criminal knowledge passing between prisoners. In the initial stages of their sentence, inmates were kept apart at all times, their faces covered by masks; they were referred to by numbers rather than names, and forbidden from talking to other prisoners. Prisoners were supposed to meditate on their wicked pasts, and the possibility of reform. It caused insanity in some prisoners; and the separate system was criticized by prison reformers, but the most significant challenges to the system were the financial costs when the prison estate expanded in the later nineteenth century.

In her mid-30s, Sarah was a relatively late starter in her criminal career. Poverty, the inability to provide for children, and/or being deserted by their husbands caused some women to start offending in their middle-ages. However, this was not the case with Sarah. She lived with a man she regarded as her husband when she was found guilty of passing off counterfeit coins. After being imprisoned for two years on that charge, she was still with her partner John Woodrow when she was further convicted of stealing sheets in Bradford and receiving another prison term (of eighteen months this time). The theft of a shirt in June 1875 meant that she faced penal servitude of seven years, followed by three years' police supervision. She started her sentence in the separate system at Wakefield, then Millbank, until that phase of her sentence ended and she was transferred to Woking Prison.

In 1876, she petitioned to get her husband's address. The reply stated that the person she asked about was not her husband and the address was not to be given to her. Initial investigations by the Bradford Police Force showed that the address that she gave for her husband (in Croft Court, Bradford), had been pulled down for railway improvements. They later stated that 'Woodrow and Smith have been living together as man and wife previous to her conviction. He is a bad character but where he at present resides we have not been able to ascertain for he only stopped one night at the address given in your letter'.

A few months later, Sarah was informed that her husband had died whilst he was serving a prison sentence at Wakefield. Sarah was given leave to write to the Chaplain at Wakefield, but not to write a private letter (that would not be read by the prison authorities) to her brother-in-law, John's brother. In 1879 she was given a conditional licence via Russell House Refuge in London with three years of her sentence unexpired. Without her partner to come back to, Sarah stayed in London and was quickly re-convicted at Surrey Sessions in 1881 for stealing coins and given seven years' penal servitude, which would be followed by another seven years police supervision.

Because she had breached her licence conditions by being convicted of this offence, she also had to serve the remainder of her first penal servitude sentence. That meant that when she was due to be released on licence, she still stayed in prison, and was only licensed when she had served another year.

On 28 October 1886 she was discharged to the care of the Discharged Prisoners' Aid Society in London; and subsequently returned back to Bradford, her home town, but sadly died in the spring of 1887.

91. Enoch Swift (born 1834, Stalybridge, Lancashire) Licence no. 93039/22606

Portland Prison (*Authors' Collections*)

Portland Prison was opened in 1848; initially the convicts who were sent there worked on the road and then on the naval dockyard and the quarries. Convicts were put to labour in groups during the day and placed in cells at night. At first cells had timber walls and were separated by corrugated iron and a shared window between cells, they measured seven feet by four feet by seven feet. As transportation ended and the prison expanded in size, by 1853 there was capacity for 1520 inmates and it was gradually rebuilt in stone. Portland was a convict prison until 1921 when it became a Borstal, more recently it has operated as a Young Offenders Institution and today it is used as a prison for adult and young offenders.

Enoch Swift was born in Lancashire in the 1830s, but during his childhood the family moved to South Yorkshire. In 1858 Enoch was charged with stealing a clock. The charge was the result of a family dispute as the clock had been won as a raffle prize, and both he and his father claimed it as their own. The magistrates dismissed the case saying they had no power to resolve the dispute.

Unfortunately this was not Enoch's only appearance in court and he was in fact going to spend the next thirty years or more before the bench for a range of offences, mostly for those relating to the Game Laws. In 1861 he was fined for trespassing in the pursuit of game and later the same year he was sentenced to twelve months for stealing boots. Enoch only received one conviction that drew him into the convict system as most of his offences were minor and this offence occurred in 1865. By this time he was married to Catherine and during 1864 they had both been in court for drunk and disorderly and theft offences.

In 1865, they both faced charges of larceny for the theft of a game cock and five hens; and Enoch was also charged with stealing two sacks and a spade. The police had searched the Swifts' home, finding the sacks and the spade and some of the fowl nearby. Catherine was acquitted, but Enoch received seven years' penal servitude. He served the period of separate confinement at Wakefield House of Correction where the government rented cells for convicts; and after a few months he was transferred to public works at Portland Prison. He worked on the quarry, his conduct was good, and he learnt to write. In October 1866 he lost forty-two remission marks for 'wrangling with another prisoner', though this was his only offence in prison. He served just under five and a half years of his sentence before being released on licence.

Enoch returned to Yorkshire and worked as an iron puddler, and for a time he may have been living apart from Catherine but they were certainly together by 1881. Enoch had also been acquitted of larceny in 1872 and fined by Rotherham magistrates in 1875 after being found guilty of trespassing in the pursuit of game.

Throughout the 1880s and 1890s Enoch continued to offend, being found guilty for game or game-related offences such as trespassing, assaulting a gamekeeper or a police constable; he was fined or served short periods in a local prison. He was a regular in court and by 1891, the *Sheffield and Rotherham Independent* described him as an 'old offender' with twenty-nine convictions for poaching before that bench and probably others as well. These were minor offences and outside of the licensing period so they did not result in his recall to the convict system.

92. Elizabeth Tankard (born 1841, Manchester) Licence no. 3776

Female convicts on laundry duty (*H. Mayhew and J. Binny*, The Criminal Prisons of London and Scenes of London Life, *1862*)

Unfortunately, there is little research on prison suicides in Victorian gaols. However, we do know that many prisoners were vulnerable; had difficult pasts to deal with; an unenviable time in prison ahead of them; and their future prospects were also poor. Little wonder that many tried to kill themselves. Suicide is still a feature of prison life today, and women are still more likely to attempt suicide in prison then men. The Victorian prison authorities appear to have paid little attention to the emotional vulnerability of their charges, and when prisoners did try and kill themselves, the attempts were often downplayed (as was the case with Elizabeth and her attempt).

Aged seventeen, Elizabeth was sentenced to six months in her home-town gaol for stealing blankets. Another month followed after she assaulted a neighbour. The Manchester Prison register described her as an unmarried servant, with a scar in the corner of each eye. In the year after her release she was arrested for stealing money, but the evidence was not strong enough to bring the case to court. In 1866, however, she was sentenced to seven years' penal servitude by Lancaster Assizes for robbery with violence: beating and assaulting John Dyson and robbing him of £3 and three shillings.

In prison she had some episodes of disorderliness in her first year of custody, but was an unremarkable prisoner in most respects. She was clearly an unhappy woman though. In 1867 she threatened to 'destroy herself' and was referred to the Medical Officer, but she was not admitted to the Prison Infirmary, nor did she receive any medical treatment. The following year the prison record stated: '…committed a feigned attempt at suicide by suspending herself by a handkerchief to the ventilator of her cell at Brixton prison'.

Today, prisoners thought to be suicidal are confined to a ligature-proof cell, and they are deprived of shoelaces, indeed anything that could be used in a hanging (even so the suicide rate in prison is unacceptably high). Elizabeth's suicide attempt prompted little reaction, the reason for this being made clear in the Medical Officer's notes: 'She is a nervous, excitable woman but without any indications of insanity'. Elizabeth's breaches of prison regulations increased after the attempted suicide, and they also changed character. She became much more disorderly and violent. She was punished for shouting, impertinence, showing temper, and disobeying direct instructions given to her by prison staff, and also having a concealed piece of steel on her person. Nevertheless, she was released on licence two years early, aged 28.

There are no further records of offending by Elizabeth, and in fact there is not much more information that can be found about this female after her release. She entered into the prison system aged seventeen and she came out nearly ten year's older (and possibly wiser). The suicide attempts may have been a cry for help, an unsuccessful attempt to manipulate the prison authorities (although it is hard to see what Elizabeth could gain by this course of action), or a genuine attempt to end her life. Whatever the real reason for her attempted self-strangulation, she survived convict prison, and managed to stay out of trouble when she left prison in 1871.

93. Ellen Terrell (born c.1844, Lambeth, London) Licence no. 3837

Horsemonger Lane Gaol Gatehouse (*H. Mayhew and J. Binny,* The Criminal Prisons and Scenes of London Life, *1862*)

Horsemonger Lane Gaol in Southwark, Surrey was built in the 1790s, during a period of 'reform' in the county gaols. When it first opened it was the largest prison in Surrey, holding around 300 inmates, both criminals and debtors and was the principle place of execution for the county. It closed in 1878 after the centralisation of local prisons. In 1849 it was the site of a famous execution when on 13 November, married couple, Maria and Frederick Manning, were both executed on the gatehouse roof, for the murder of Maria's lover, Patrick O'Connor. The execution was attended by Charles Dickens who immediately wrote a letter to *The Times* about the 'wickedness and levity' of the crowd who attended public executions.

Ellen Terrell was born in the early to mid-1840s. Aged 7, she was recorded on the 1851 Census as a 'visitor' to William and Isabella London, who resided in Tower Hamlets, Whitechapel, having been born in St Luke's, Middlesex. Whether these people were her relations is unclear as the census ten years later records Ellen residing in a lodging house in Southwark, though her place of birth is then recorded as Surrey.

A couple of years later, Ellen began to commit crime; she served six months in prison in 1863, twelve months in 1865 and a further three months for a summary conviction in the autumn of 1866. These previous convictions were taken into account when she was found guilty of receiving stolen money in March 1867. The Surrey Quarter Sessions sentenced her to seven years' penal servitude. Ellen had been committed to Horsemonger Lane Gaol in February 1867. At the time of her committal she had an infant child and was therefore held 'in association' and not separate confinement. No children were permitted in the convict prison system and so infants like Ellen's were removed from their mothers' and sent to family, friends or sent to Industrial Schools. Babies were only present in the local prison system and women sentenced to penal servitude were permitted to stay with them for a short period in a local prison; and then they were sent down to the convict prisons without them.

Ellen was transferred to Millbank in June 1867 where she underwent the separation period of her sentence and worked in the laundry. She was then transferred to Brixton in November 1867 for public works and continued to work in the laundry. On Christmas Day she was punished for 'loud singing and shouting', placed in close confinement for one day and forfeited twenty-eight remission marks. She was punished again in June and August 1868 at Brixton and spent another couple of days in close confinement; and lost a further fifty-six remission marks for insolence and other offences. Throughout her imprisonment she wrote and received letters and she was visited (despite the census information which reveals little about her family), so she did have support outside prison from someone. It may have been her brother 'Mich', who was recorded as her next of kin on the Penal Record and who lived in Angel Place, Borough.

After being transferred to Woking and then onto Fulham Refuge, where she undertook needlework, Ellen received a conditional licence and was sent to Battery House Refuge in June 1871. She would have been released after a six to nine months at the refuge. Ellen did not commit any further offences during her lifetime but we lose track of her when she leaves prison.

94. Edward Vidler (born 1820, Newgate, London) Licence no. 121

Newgate was London's main prison in the eighteenth century, and was still an important part of the penal system in the nineteenth. It housed many famous prisoners, such as William Cobbett, the agrarian activist, author William Defoe, Jack Shepherd (who escaped), and may thousands of run-of-the-mill prisoners. Hangings took place outside the prison before 1868, when the last public execution took place outside its walls. Thereafter the gallows was removed to inside the prison, where capital sentences still took place for many years. The prison was closed in 1902, demolished two years later, and the Old Bailey now stands on the site of the old prison.

The gatehouse of Newgate Prison
(*Authors' Collections*)

Somewhat ironically, Edward was born in 1820 close to Newgate Prison, which would be his future home for a brief unhappy period. His parents were coal merchants and Edward probably played a part in their business activities as he was used to handling orders. However, he fell foul of business practices when he was convicted at the Old Bailey in 1848 of financial fraud. The large amount involved, forging a document ordering £350 of goods, ensured a hefty sentence, and he was sentenced to penal servitude for ten years. He was deposited in the hulk, *Defence*, moored in the River Thames. The *Defence* was a decommissioned Royal Naval third-rate ship of the line which became a prison ship when she was found to be unsuitable for military service. At various points it was used as a secure convict invalid depot, and it kept Edward until he was well enough to be transferred to the hulk, *Stirling Castle* (another former third-rate Royal Navy ship of the line).

Like many others sentenced in the 1850s, although sentenced to be transported to Australia, he never actually sailed on that fateful journey. He served all his time on hulks, until released on a ticket-of-leave in 1853. He had almost half of his sentence remitted, nearly five years, with the condition that he did not consort with thieves and prostitutes, and, of course, did not commit any further offences. However, Edward did not stay out of trouble for long.

Within six months of his release he committed a similar offence to the one which had landed him in trouble some years earlier. He was convicted of forging a cheque purporting to have been legitimately signed by Lieutenant Colonel Jebb of the Royal Engineers and sentenced at the Old Bailey to another ten years' sentence of penal servitude. It actually appears that he wanted to be transported to Van Diemen's Land, and pleaded with the judge that, this time, he would be sent their straight away rather than spend time on a hulk. He never made it to Australia, however, for the tragic reason that he died very shortly after being sentenced.

Let us return for a moment to the victim of his last fraud. Joshua Jebb held an army rank in 1854, but he is much more well-known as the first Director of Convict Prisons. Appointed in 1850, he held the post for over a decade, during which time he oversaw the decline of mass convict transportation, and the growth of the British convict penal estate. It is unlikely that Edward recognised Jebb's name when he was forging it, but it is hard to think of a more unsuitable victim to try and con.

95. George Warwick (born 1854, Newfoundland) Licence no. 58172

One of the most famous escapees from London prisons was Jack Shepherd, the notorious eighteenth-century burglar. He was imprisoned five times in 1724 but escaped on four separate occasions, making him a notorious public and extremely popular figure, especially with the London laboring classes. He was caught, convicted, and met his end at the Tyburn gallows. He only troubled the authorities for two years, but for the audacity of his escape attempts, he came to feature in many cultural productions, including a faux autobiography (probably written by Daniel Defoe); and as the character (Macheath) in *The Beggar's Opera*, written in 1725 by John Gay.

Jack Sheppard in Newgate Prison
(*Public Domain*)

George was convicted at Birkenhead of shop-breaking with another 16 year-old at Tranmere in 1870. His parents Jane and George Warwick Senior were convicted of handling and receiving goods they had stolen. And not for the first time; for when the police arrested the parents they were found in possession of a number of pawnbroker's tickets. The two boys were implicated in a number of other robberies, and George had only just been released from gaol three weeks before committing this offence. That time he had been convicted alongside his mother of three burglaries of beef and wine from local hotels. George's father was possibly absent from that 'job' because he was still in prison for earlier thefts committed with son – he still had four months to go on that sentence.

So, the whole family were used to serving short prison sentences, but in 1871, George was convicted of 'larceny after previous felony' at Knutsford Quarter Sessions, and sentenced to seven years' penal servitude; and a further seven years' police supervision. His co-defendant (his mother Jane) received a twelve-month sentence. So whilst she remained in a local prison, George was sent to Brixton convict prison. He was 'at large' again in 1876, when he was released on licence to the Royal Prisoners' Aid Society in London.

He did not stay there long, but enlisted in the 21st Hussars. He was still in the army and still on licence when he was convicted at Middlesex Sessions for larceny. He had stolen a wallet from a naval captain who had bought him a drink when sheltering from the rain at the horse races at Littleton Park (now Shepperton BBC Studios) which was not far from his barracks in Hounslow. He received ten years' penal servitude and seven years' police supervision.

George suffered from chronic heart conditions in prison, so an *emplast belladonna* (a medical treatment which uses deadly nightshade) was administered in 1878 for his *morbis cordis* (heart disease or angina), but this did not stop him from a dramatic break for freedom. Breaking away whilst carrying breakfast from the kitchen to the Lunatic Wing, he scaled the intimidating prison wall and escaped. He also resisted the officer that recaptured him about four miles from the prison.

For his escape attempt he lost remission, was put to 'crank' (a revolving disc to which pressure was applied by the prisoner as a punishment), kept in cross irons, and dressed in 'parte-coloured' clothes so as to denote him as a prison-breaker. Seven days after his escape he was transferred from Woking to Portland, but he was only allowed back in normal prison-wear in January 1880. In the following years his heart condition worsened, and he was licensed in 1887 with just one month of his sentence unserved. He died in Shoreditch in 1891, aged just 37.

96. Ellen Whaling (born c.1836, Tipperary, Ireland) Licence no. 85335/7539

Prestwich or Lancashire Lunatic Asylum was opened in 1851, at first the hospital accommodated 500 patients, though it was extended in 1863 for a further 560 patients. In 1884 an Annex was built for a further 1,100 patients and by 1903 the institution could hold up to 3,135 patients from the region. About half of those admitted recovered and left the hospital, though those that remained were admitted for a variety of reasons such as poverty, illness or pregnancy outside of wedlock. Some patients stayed for decades and died in the hospital, over 5,000 patients were buried in unmarked graves due to pauper funerals at the nearby St Mary's CE Church and there is now a memorial to them.

Ellen Whaling
(*The National Archives*)

Ellen Whaling spent most of her life in and out of various institutions in the north west of England and the Midlands. She was born in Tipperary, Ireland, though it is not clear when she moved to England; her siblings were in America and she appeared to be alone.

At 23 years old Ellen was admitted to Prestwich Lunatic Asylum; she was recorded as single, childless and was a domestic servant. It is not clear when she left the asylum but in 1866 she served eighteen months in Stafford Prison for assault and robbery. Her early history is patchy, but she may have spent time in Withington Workhouse, Manchester in 1870. In 1871 she was back in Prestwich Asylum, though out a year later, as in the next few years she was convicted of various summary offences: for drunkenness, threatening language, and assault; and she served short periods in Manchester and Stafford prisons, though she was found not guilty of larceny at Knutsford in 1874. She was a 'hawker' (a mobile trader) and clearly moved around the region.

Ellen entered the convict system in 1875, she was convicted of stealing ten shillings from George Allmark and sentenced to seven years' penal servitude. She entered Knutsford House of Correction and was then sent to Millbank, where she worked knitting in her cell. She had a speech impediment as part of her palate and the back of her nose was missing. In May 1876 she moved to Woking Prison; and for having an extra pair of stockings she lost twenty-eight remission marks; for being defiant when told to clean the ward, she was confined to her cell for two days, was refused permission to clean for a month and lost twelve remission marks. She also quarrelled and struck another prisoner, losing her berth in the workroom; and in April 1879 she was rude when challenged by staff at dinner, put on a bread and water diet and lost twelve remission marks.

Three months later, she was released on conditional licence to the East End Refuge with three years and one month of her sentence unexpired. Ellen left the refuge in April 1880 and returned to Liverpool, as she was working as a domestic servant in 1881. During 1882 she was sent to Stafford Prison for fourteen days, for obscene language. In July 1883 she was convicted at Liverpool of larceny having stolen a purse and £6 at Widnes; she was sentenced to five years' penal servitude and police supervision. She was received at Millbank and then sent on to Woking where she was put to light labour; but in February 1886 was moved to Fulham Prison.

Ellen was released in November 1886 on licence and sent to the Discharged Prisoners' Aid Society (DPAS) for support. She was boarding in a house in Manchester in 1891 but in the following years returned to Prestwich Asylum as she was there in 1901; and still there in 1911 when she was 75 years old.

97. George Whitehood (born 1846, unknown) Licence no. 89418/22493

Transportation to Australia had resulted in over 168,000 men, women and children as young as nine years old being forcibly exiled from the shores of Britain. However, by the 1860s, not only was transportation becoming unpopular both as a punishment and with the free settlers in Australia, but gold had been discovered in the country. The largest gold nugget ever found in the world (yielding over 70kg of gold) was nicknamed the 'Welcome Stranger', and found in Victoria in February 1869. Such finds meant that it was no longer difficult to encourage prospective colonists to Australia, thereby helping both to hasten the end of transportation and the development of the convict prison system in Britain.

The 'Welcome Stranger' nugget
(*Authors' Collections*)

George Whitehood (aka Whitehead) only appeared a couple of times in criminal justice records. At the age of 23 he was tried, along with Charles Holden (34 years of age) at the Old Bailey with setting fire to three stacks of wheat valued at £450, the property of farmer Matthew Newman, at Cold Harbour Farm near Hayes, Middlesex on 8 October 1869.

This appeared at first sight to be a straightforward case of arson, but things were not quite as they appeared. Not one of the numerous witnesses who had seen Holden loitering about the farm recalled catching so much as a glimpse of George Whitehood at the scene of the crime. Whilst Holden was caught red-handed with 'six Lucifer matches' in his pocket, and stated that he 'may as well be in prison as starving', Whitehood called at the local police station three days later, insisting that he was the guilty man. The police officer was obviously sceptical about Whitehood's claim, stating that Whitehood 'could give no account of himself, and it was believed his intellect was affected'.

The same officer also stated that Whitehood 'was only liberated from the gaol at Wandsworth at 9.30 on the morning of the fire, and could not have walked the distance in the time'. Whitehood had been sentenced to three weeks' imprisonment in Wandsworth for an unspecified offence heard at Croydon magistrates in mid–September. It looked as though Whitehood was a troubled young man with mental issues.

However, the judge at his trial (which was postponed for a week whilst enquiries were made) saw things somewhat differently. He was of the belief that Whitehood had confessed to the crime in order to get himself transported (obviously not realising that such a sentence was no longer handed out) and that he (the judge) feared that if he were released 'he would commit some great crime in order to get what he wanted, unless before he were discharged some changes were wrought in him'. Enquiries suggested that Whitehood was 'perfectly sane' and that 'he had been branded as a deserter'. He was subsequently sentenced to ten years' penal servitude at the Old Bailey on 25 October 1869.

Regardless of Whitehood's degree of sanity, it was quickly realised that this sentence was an abuse of judicial power, and efforts were put in place to release Whitehood from HMP Brixton. On 30 July 1870 a letter from the Home Office to the Governor of Brixton contained a licence for Whitehood's imminent release, with a caveat stating that 'if he commits another offence it will subject him to imprisonment in and not removal from this country'. On 15 August 1870 Whitehood was released on licence, after spending ten months in prison for an offence that he clearly did not commit.

98. Elizabeth Williams (born 1848, Stafford) Licence no. 3729

The convict prison was a tightly controlled space, with a fixed timetable of events (breakfast, work time, exercise period, lights out, and so on) rigorously enforced. Behaviour within the prison was also very strictly monitored. Not surprisingly, the vast majority of prisoners could not always keep to these tight controls. Some, like Elizabeth, contravened the regulations many times. When they breached the rules by talking without permission, stealing, fighting with prisoners, disobeying or cheeking staff and so on, punishments included the loss of remission, a poorer diet, or physical restriction in a canvas dress, cross-irons or straitjacket.

Convict chain room, Millbank Prison
(*H. Mayhew and J. Binny*, The Criminal Prisons of London and Scenes of London Life, *1862*)

Still in her late teens, Elizabeth Williams was sentenced in April 1865 to seven years' penal servitude by Staffordshire Quarter Sessions (for larceny). She was the daughter of a master bricklayer who employed four men in 1861 in Castle Church, Staffordshire. The family lived in Bilston near Wolverhampton when Elizabeth was taken to court.

Elizabeth started her prison life in Millbank, before being deposited in Brixton (the main female convict prison). She resisted the system at every turn, breaking window panes and disobeying orders given to her by warders at the start of her prison term. Her resistance did not wane as her sentence progressed. For example, in 1868, she was disciplined for the following: calling the director vile names on passing from the office to her cell after having an interview with him; assaulting an officer; destroying prison property; using bad language to the chaplain, throwing water over her officer and destroying prison property; bad language; shouting and insolence; acting disorderly; assaulting an officer; having writing materials in her cell; destroying prison property; refusing to go to her ward (and again refusing to go to her ward a few days later); bad language; refusing to leave the ward; and, lastly, on 18

November, 'threatening to take the life of the deputy superintendent and assaulting an officer on two occasions'.

This was her forty-third prison offence, and the authorities removed her from Brixton to Millbank. Possibly the repeated use of handcuffs, cross-irons, and physical restraints, together with a large number of days on a bread and water (penal diet) had a cumulative effect. At Millbank she was considered too weak to endure a penal diet, or to continue her prison work.

She was then rotated back and forth between the Millbank and Brixton establishments, where she again regularly breached prison regulations. After being disciplined for talking in the prison yard; laughing and shouting; laughing and playing about in the prison chapel; destroying her prison clothes and so on, she was released on licence one year and three months before her sentence expired. She had lost a good deal of remission, but her behaviour in prison did not prohibit her early release.

Why had she reacted so defiantly to the prison regime? It appears that she may have felt abandoned to a pretty dismal life. Her parents never wrote to her whilst she was in prison, nor she to them. She spent six years in a convict prison, and that term must have stretched out seemingly endlessly when she entered prison for the first time as an 18-year-old girl. Once she had attracted a reputation for opposition, presumably she was subject to closer attention, and a vicious circle of offending inside prison continued. She only, it must be remembered, ever committed one single theft in the whole of her life.

99. James Woodhouse (born c.1851, Morecambe) Licence no. A37318/ 45255

Victorian bust of a judge
(*Authors' Collections*)

Before men and women could divorce on equal terms and without blame being apportioned, bigamy was seen as one way in which men (or less usually, women) could evade an unhappy and sometimes dangerous marriage and begin afresh. Bigamy was first made a felony in 1603, and as such was theoretically punishable by death. However, this sentence was very rarely imposed; most offenders such as Woodhouse received a term of imprisonment. Judicial discretion was often utilised, with many judges realising that a bigamous relationship, following a mutually agreed separation of married couples, was, until the laws surrounding divorce were relaxed, the only way in which men and women could restart their lives. Long terms of penal servitude were normally reserved for serial bigamists whose infidelity was not down to love, but to fraudulent behaviour.

James Woodhouse married Esther Ann Bennett in the summer of 1872 at Blackburn and by 1881 he and Esther had produced three boys; and had moved to Barrow in Furness, where he worked as an engine driver. However, two years later, this picture of apparent domestic harmony was shattered when he appeared at Manchester Assizes, charged with bigamy at Accrington. The judge is reported as stating that 'this was one of the most shocking cases he had come across, a young woman having been duped, plundered and [...] might be ruined by the prisoner'. Woodhouse had courted Frances Jane Ling Taylor, a butcher's daughter, under an assumed name, and subsequently married her. He had then deserted her, claiming that he had to join a sailing ship. He 'got from her some of her rings and trinkets' and fled the scene.

No reason is known as to why Woodhouse suddenly behaved this way, but he was sentenced to five years' penal servitude and on 7 March 1883 he entered through the gates of Strangeways Prison. He was classified as a 'Star Class' prisoner i.e. a first offender and one who was thought unlikely to cause any trouble whilst serving his sentence. Such 'Star Class' offenders were largely segregated from the more hardened recidivists in order to prevent them being tainted by association. His conduct prior to entering prison was described in a report on character and way of life as 'good – worked at print works as mechanic labourer then as engine driver, regular in mode and habit, good character friends'.

During the whole period of his imprisonment James maintained a regular correspondence with his parents and only broke prison regulations on one occasion – when he was caught talking to another prisoner whilst sorting rags – for which he was kept in close confinement for a day, gained 240 additional marks against his character and lost thirty remission marks. He moved around the prison estate, serving his sentence in Pentonville, Chatham and Chattenden (near Rochester). In 1884 he petitioned the Home Secretary on grounds of mercy, claiming that he had been led into bigamy, but his petition was refused. However, on 24 March 1887 he was released on licence and he returned to Lancashire.

His wife Esther seems to have stuck by him and there must have been a reconciliation soon after his release as is the 1891 census he is recorded as a blacksmith living in Rishton, near Blackburn, with his wife Esther and six children, including 3-year-old Agnes. The marriage lasted until at least 1911 when he and his wife appear in the census as still living in Blackburn. He died in Blackburn in 1927, eight years before his wife.

100. Mary Wright (born 1853, Bonsall, Derbyshire) Licence no. 95783/ 7604

> *Clause 2 does away with the empanelling of a special jury of twelve matrons to try whether or not the woman is with child. I have no doubt that in the past such a procedure had a purpose, but it is really unnecessary nowadays. It dates from a time when it was not usual for an experienced medical official always to be present in Court. As your Lordships are well aware, in modern times a doctor is always in Court.*

Sentence of Death (expectant mothers) Bill, Second reading, 18 June 1931 (*Lord Chancellor Sankey*)

Mary grew up in a respectable family in Derbyshire, her father being a local farmer and grocer. Just out of her teens, she became pregnant (the father was rumoured to be one of her father's farm hands). Her illegitimate daughter Adeline (known as Addie) stayed with her in the family home. It looked as though Addie would be joined by a little brother or sister in 1880 when Mary again became pregnant (again, the local rumour was that the same man, Henry Abell, was the father). The disgrace of having two illegitimate grandchildren was too much to bear for Mary's father, and he asked Mary to leave his house.

In the period when women were still capitally sentenced it was considered manifestly unjust for pregnant women to be hanged, since an innocent child would suffer along with its mother. In order to ascertain whether a woman was 'quick with child', a selection of women (known as a 'Jury of Matrons') drawn from the crowd watching the trial were commissioned to examine the female defendant. Women who successfully 'pleaded their belly' had their death sentence postponed or had it commuted into penal servitude. A Jury of Matrons was rarely convened after the eighteenth century ended, and the last examination took place in 1914, with the whole practice being abolished in 1931.

One night in July 1880 Mary knocked on a neighbour's door and asked if she could come in. Her clothes were soaked and the neighbour questioned why Mary was holding Adeline's blue bonnet in her wet hands. When Mary replied that the three-year old child was left in the mere, her father, and later a police officer were called. Her father fished Adeline out from the water. Although the coroner later reported that she had not been long in the mere, she was quite dead. Mary's mother burst into tears when she learned of the tragic event, but Mary simply replied that it was not her mother's fault, it was all at her own hands. She had meant to drown both of them in the mere, as she had heard that drowning was a simple thing, but despite standing in the water for two hours, she found herself alive, and her child deceased.

The case aroused a lot of sympathy in the local area (Matlock and Buxton), not least because Mary cut a pathetic figure in the dock, and was known to be 'simple minded'. The jury in her trial requested that she be shown mercy. The judge, clearly sympathetic himself, pronounced the death sentence but forewent the traditional black cap. He recommended mercy to the Home Office, and Mary's sentence was commuted to ten years' penal servitude. His recommendation was well-supported by the fact that a Jury of Matrons had confirmed that Mary was pregnant with a second child, which would now be born in prison. Mary served her time in Millbank and Woking prisons, where she suffered indifferent health. In May 1886 Mary's brother sent a petition to the Home Secretary on behalf of Mary due to her poor health and asking for his support. By August he had enlisted the support of his local MP, who also wrote to the Home Office. Mary was released on licence in March 1887, with nearly four years unserved on her sentence, and she never re-offended.

Perhaps the saddest thing about this case is that the Governor of Millbank wrote on her prison record: 'I believe a Jury of Matrons at her trial confirmed her statement that she was with child. There were not any signs of pregnancy when she came here in March 1881'. Mary need never have taken that fateful decision in 1880.

Conclusion

What happened to the convict prisons that we have been describing? In 1877 the local prisons housing minor offenders, which had previously been controlled by local authorities, and the convict prisons for those undergoing penal servitude, were brought together and placed under the control of the Prison Commission (ultimately responsible to the Home Secretary). The new improved prison system came under sustained criticism in the 1890s, and as a result the 1895 Gladstone Report ushered in a more liberal regime for the British penal estate.

The convict prisons of the Victorian period were supposed to be next only to death in terms of experience. However, by 1930, a reforming Prisons Commissioner, Alexander Paterson, promoted the view that men were sent to prison *as* a punishment, not *for* punishment. Many of the harsh conditions imposed in the last hundred years were gradually removed or reduced in severity. Of course convicts were still locked up in pretty poor conditions, with restricted diets, and they still heard the cell door slam each night, locking them up with their fellow prisoners in overcrowded cells. However, prison conditions were now designed to keep violent and dishonest people away from respectable society, not grind them into submission with hard labour and physical discipline.

In 1898 the strict rules of silence were removed, and the crank and treadwheel (both unproductive labour originally intended to instil discipline and the ethics of hard work into convicts) were also removed at the same time. From 1921 prisoners were no longer subject to having their hair cropped (they could even grow beards if they wished) and the broad arrow symbol was removed from prison uniform. After another report, published in 1922, also criticized outdated penal methods and the lack of humanity in the system, another wave of reform followed. Flogging as a disciplinary tool was abandoned in 1922 (though the last birching of a prisoner took place as late as 1962); and the separation of prisoners was suspended in 1923 and abolished in 1924. In the same year prisoners were not required to attend religious services; and those thought capable of escape were no longer required to walk in chains or wear *parte-coloured* prison clothes (which are described earlier in this book).

The First World War had seen the number of prisoners fall (many minor offenders had already been taken out of the system by the introduction of probation as a non-custodial option in 1908), and the depression of the 1930s put severe financial pressure on the whole prison system. Many prisons were closed. Many others crammed prisoners together in a system which started to creak. After the Second World War, conditions deteriorated even further, although the distinction between convict prisons and other prisons was ended as a result of the 1948 Criminal Justice Act, which also abolished hard labour. Post-war governments did not want to invest in better penal conditions, even if they had the means to do so. Despite the attempts of groups such as the Howard League, many prisons returned to the kind of state that Victorian philanthropists and reformers had campaigned so strongly against. Overcrowding became severe; the practice of 'slopping out' continued until 1996 because the cells and cell-blocks lacked sanitary arrangements; the prisons were cold in the winter (even in summer); educational classes were abandoned; and the prison estate was generally in a very dilapidated state.

In an attempt to manage prisoners better Lord Mountbatten's *Report* published in the 1960s persuaded the government to establish categories of prison (from Category A [for the most serious of offenders] to Category D for prisoners who went to open prisons). This reduced costs and allowed the prison authorities to upgrade the prisons that housed the most serious offenders. The report had been prompted by a series of prison escapes, and Category A prisons now became much more secure. They also became much more oppressive, and possibly for this reason, the 1970s and 1980s saw a wave of prison riots and disturbances. The Conservative administrations of the 1980s and 1990s saw this as a result of the liberal regime, not the overbearing discipline of the system. The Home Secretary of the time famously declared that 'Prison Works', and he managed the prison service much more directly, ousting the Director General of the Prison Service,

Prisoners being released from gaol
(*H. Mayhew and J. Binny*, The Criminal Prisons of London and Scenes of London Life, *1862*)

Derek Lewis, in 1995, and initiating tougher conditions for prisoners. Sentences got longer, overcrowding returned, and criminologists began to talk of the 'warehousing' of the poor. Both Conservative and Labour administrations oversaw an increase in the number of people imprisoned. An emphasis on law and order and the ability of the prison to solve social problems saw the numbers of prisoners break new records throughout the 2000s (the prison population reached over 80,000, pushing the prison estate to its very limits).

Private prisons built in the late twentieth- and early twenty-first century relieved the pressure somewhat, albeit at a cost, but most of the prison estate of the late twentieth century was largely made up of prisons built in the nineteenth century. Only in the twenty-first century were prisons such as Shrewsbury (originally built in 1773, and rebuilt in 1877) and Gloucester (built in 1840) eventually closed. Some former prisons remain in business but house different guests (such as Oxford Prison, now a prestigious Malmaison hotel). This book has introduced you to some of the inhabitants of convict prisons before such establishments were either turned into luxury hotels or demolished and has hopefully given you some insights into their often desperately poor and sad lives.

Select Bibliography

Brodie, Allan, et al, *English Prisons: an Architectural History* (London: English Heritage, 2002)

Cox, David J., *Crime in England 1688–1815* (London: Routledge [*History of Crime in the UK and Ireland series*], 2014)

Godfrey, Barry, *Crime in England 1880-1945: The rough and the criminal, the policed and the incarcerated* (London: Routledge [*History of Crime in the UK and Ireland series*], 2013)

Godfrey, Barry, David J. Cox and Stephen Farrall, *Criminal Lives: Family Life, Employment, and Offending (Clarendon Criminology Series*, Oxford University Press, 2007)

Godfrey, Barry, David J. Cox and Stephen Farrall, *Serious Offenders: A Historical Study of Habitual Criminals (Clarendon Criminology Series*, Oxford University Press, 2010)

Johnston, Helen, *Crime in England 1815-1880: Experiencing the criminal justice system* (London: Routledge [*History of Crime in the UK and Ireland series*], 2015)

Marston, Edward, *Prison: Five hundred years of life behind bars* (Kew: TNA, 2009)

Storey, Neil R., *Prisons and Prisoners in Victorian Britain* (Stroud: The History Press, 2010)

Notes

1. *Report on the discipline and management of the convict prisons, and disposal of convicts, 1853,* London: HMSO, 1854, p. 17
2. 1895 [C.7702] [C.7702-I] Prisons committee. Report from the departmental committee on prisons (London: HMSO, 1895), p. 391.
3. *Report on the discipline and management of the convict prisons, and disposal of convicts, 1853,* London: HMSO, 1854, p. 20.
4. Ibid, p. 29.
5. Ibid, p. 26.
6. Ibid, p.32.
7. Ibid, p. 31.
8. 1878-79 [C.2368] [C.2368-I] [C.2368-II] Penal Servitude Acts Commission. Report of the commissioners appointed to inquire into the working of the penal servitude acts (London: HMSO, 1878), p. 358.
9. 1895 [C.7702] [C.7702-I] Prisons committee. Report from the departmental committee on prisons. (London: HMSO, 1895), p. 393.